HOW THE FUTURE BEGAN

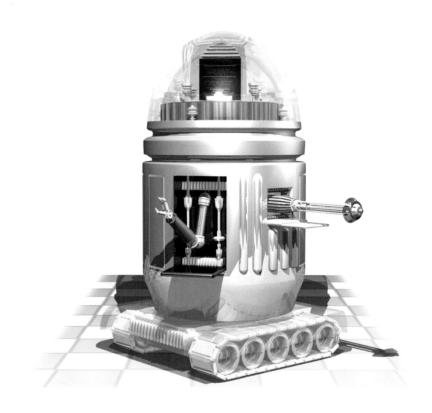

MACHINES

CLIVE GIFFORD

KINGfISHER

NEW YORK

HOW THE FUTURE BEGAN

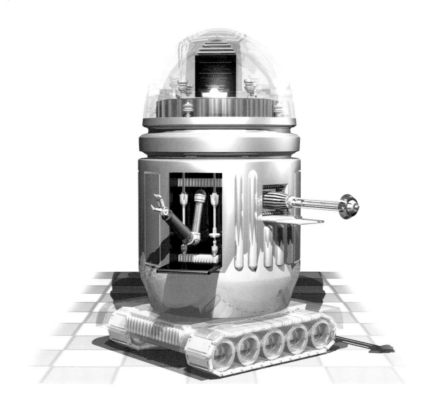

MACHINES

CLIVE GIFFORD

KINGfISHER

NEW YORK

Author
Clive Gifford

Senior Editor
Clive Wilson

Senior Designer
Mike Buckley

DTP Coordinator
Nicky Studdart

Senior Production Controller
Caroline Jackson

Picture Research Manager
Jane Lambert

Picture Researcher
Juliet Duff

Indexer
Sue Lightfoot

KINGFISHER
Larousse Kingfisher Chambers Inc.
95 Madison Avenue
New York, New York 10016

First published in 1999
1 3 5 7 9 10 8 6 4 2

1SCH/0600/TWP/RNB(RNB)/135NYMA

LIBRARY OF CONGRESS CATALOGING–IN–PUBLICATION DATA
Gifford, Clive.
How the future began. Machines / by Clive Gifford.—1st ed.
p. cm.
Summary: A guide to historical and current developments in the
field of machinery, including mass production, computers, robots,
micro-engineering, and communications technology.
1. Machinery—Juvenile literature. [1. Machinery.] I. Title.
TJ147.G53 1999 621.8—dc21 98-53274 CIP AC

ISBN 0-7534-5188-3
Printed in Singapore

CONTENTS

INTRODUCTION   6

MACHINES IN INDUSTRY
Introduction   8
Robots at Work   10
Smart Factories   12
Micromachines   14
Nanotechnology   16
New Materials   18

CREATING POWER
Introduction   20
Fossil Fuels   22
Energy from Atoms   24
Energy from the Cores   26
Harnessing the Elements   28
Greater Efficiency   30

MILITARY MACHINES
Introduction   32
Spying and Defense   34
Personal Weapons   36
Delivery Systems   38
Future Battlegrounds   40

MACHINES NEAR AND FAR
Introduction   42
In the Home   44
Domestic Robots   46
Shopping and Banking   48
Machines in Hazardous Areas   50
Underwater Machines   52
Machines in Space 1   54
Machines in Space 2   56
Our New Home   58

REFERENCE
Glossary   60
Websites/Places of Interest   61

Index   62
Acknowledgments   64

It is almost impossible to imagine a world without machines. Cars, aircraft, computers, factories, and communication networks have transformed almost every aspect of our lives. Machines have helped us to move faster and work more efficiently, as well as giving us more free time. They have taken us underwater and into space—journeys we could once only dream of. Where machines will take us in the future is limited only by our imagination.

Ever since our ancestors first used stone tools, humans have been using machines. For most of history, machines were simple devices that channeled mechanical force supplied by humans or animals. Then, in the 1700s, the invention of the steam engine kickstarted the Industrial Revolution and propelled us into a new era—one dominated by increasingly sophisticated and powerful machines.

During the 21st century, advances in computer technology will make machines smarter and even more powerful. Many machines will function with a minimum of human intervention. Robot carers will look after the sick, remote vehicles will explore hazardous places, and tiny robots will perform delicate surgery deep inside the body. In the more distant future, machines may even enable the human race to colonize other planets.

Some of the predictions made in this book may not happen, while other unexpected developments may occur. But one thing is certain—machines will continue to flourish and shape our future.

1970s
Use of composite materials, e.g. in fighter aircraft

1960s
Early development of smart materials

1961
First industrial robot, built by Unimation

1908
First mass production assembly line

1903
Development of stainless steel

1767
Spinning jenny first machine to spin many threads at a time

1728
Falcon's loom uses punch card system

MACHINES IN INDUSTRY

People have been using machines ever since the first prehistoric human scraped an animal hide with a sharpened flint edge, or moved a large rock with a stick as a lever. Machines have developed in complexity as we have learned how to use and control aspects of the world around us—from making and shaping materials such as metals to manipulating forces such as electricity and air pressure.

The 20th century saw a revolution in the way many people work. Much of that is due to machines, from the rise of mass production in factories with its dependence on machines and automation, to the invention of the computer, which has transformed millions of jobs. In the 21st century, humans will supervise robots and automated machine workers, often from far away, as the remote, automated factory becomes a reality. With giant leaps in nanotechnology and microengineering, communications technology and new materials, the products of the future may not only be very different from today's, but may also be manufactured in completely new ways.

1988
First use of robots in nuclear power plants

1990s
First molecular machines designed

2006
Smart metal alloys used for domestic objects

2008
Fully dextrous multipurpose robot in use

2015
VR and automation allow customization via remote factories

2060
Nanorobots used in surgery

ROBOTS AT WORK

Although there are currently thousands of robots at work all over the world, robotics—the study, design, and improvement of robots—is still in its infancy. Even so, many robots perform tasks that are impossible for humans and do some jobs more quickly and accurately than us. However, developments in robotics are expected to happen, creating far more flexible, versatile, and affordable machines that will be able to work with little or no human intervention. Whatever the speed of development, one thing is certain—our dependence on robots is only going to increase as we move further into the 21st century.

△ Automatons, like this model carriage, are machines that simulate realistic activity.

What is a robot?

There is no one perfect definition of a robot. It is fair to say, however, that it is an automated machine that performs some humanlike actions, and reacts to certain external events as well as to preprogrammed instructions. A robot does not have to look like a human. Robots are built to designs that are most suited to their work. If a robot is going to work in only one place, for example, it does not need legs or a system to move around.

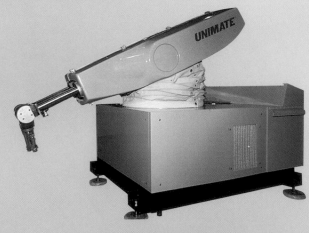

△ The Unimate robot is a direct descendant of the very first robot arm—a machine that first handled hot metal die-casting in 1961.

△ The word "robot" featured in a 1922 play called *Rossum's Universal Robots,* by Karel Čapek. It comes from the Czech word meaning "forced labor."

Intelligent glimmers

Early robots were extremely good at repeating an identical operation time after time. New generations of robots, equipped with high-resolution vision systems and complex object recognition will be able to adjust and adapt to a greater range of work scenarios. By 2030, robots are likely to be equipped with advanced "fuzzy logic" circuits. These will help them make decisions in keeping with the complexities and problems of the real world.

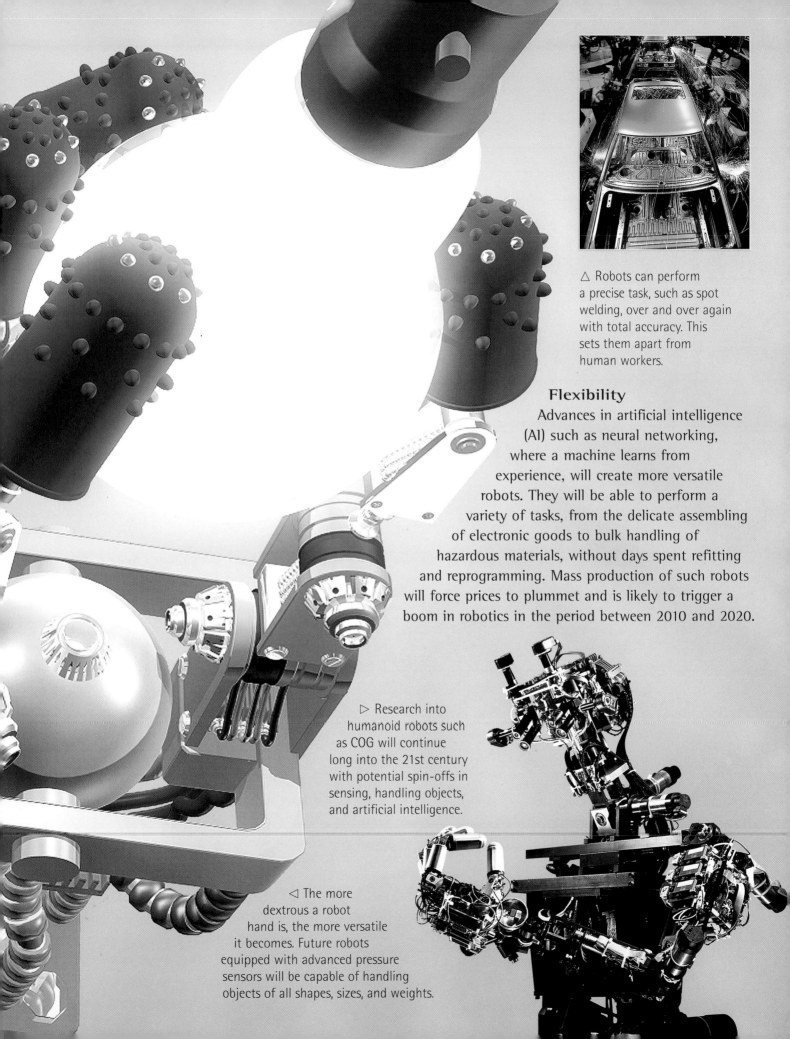

△ Robots can perform a precise task, such as spot welding, over and over again with total accuracy. This sets them apart from human workers.

Flexibility

Advances in artificial intelligence (AI) such as neural networking, where a machine learns from experience, will create more versatile robots. They will be able to perform a variety of tasks, from the delicate assembling of electronic goods to bulk handling of hazardous materials, without days spent refitting and reprogramming. Mass production of such robots will force prices to plummet and is likely to trigger a boom in robotics in the period between 2010 and 2020.

▷ Research into humanoid robots such as COG will continue long into the 21st century with potential spin-offs in sensing, handling objects, and artificial intelligence.

◁ The more dextrous a robot hand is, the more versatile it becomes. Future robots equipped with advanced pressure sensors will be capable of handling objects of all shapes, sizes, and weights.

SMART FACTORIES

The Industrial Revolution in Europe in the 18th and 19th centuries altered the way most people had been working for thousands of years. Time-consuming work by individuals was replaced by factories that grouped together large numbers of people and machinery. During the 20th century, assembly lines, automation, and early industrial robots increased productivity and made it possible to manufacture great numbers of affordable products. The smart factory of the 21st century will make products even more easily available and cheaper to buy. Smart factories will depend on advances in artificial intelligence, robotics, and automation processes to create factories that can function with almost no human involvement.

△ Working conditions in factories of the 1800s were often dirty, cramped, and dangerous. People were forced to perform boring, repetitive tasks for hours on end.

▷ Automatic guided vehicles (AGVs) transport materials and parts between automated processes. Here, an AGV ferries a car shell along an assembly line in Turin, Italy.

◁ Completely automated factories will feature self-checking equipment, maintenance robots, and computer networks that constantly check that the factory is running smoothly.

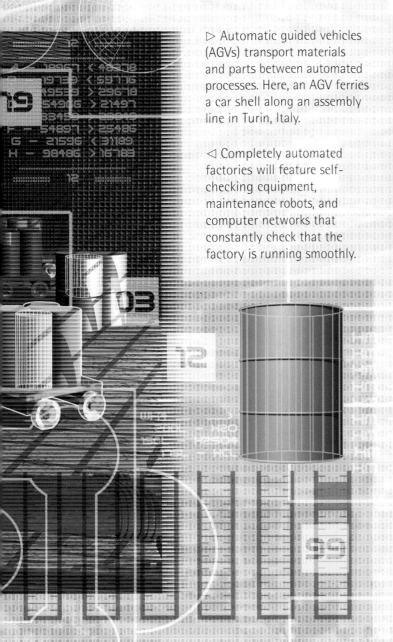

Remote factories

By 2030, smart factories will be able to operate with a minimum of human help. These factories will feature self-checking equipment, robot maintenance and repair, and a mixture of software and robot supervision. Unlike factories of the past, they will not need to be located near large towns, which in earlier times would have provided the workforce. Instead, they may be built in remote sites or near raw material sources.

Consumer power

With competition even more intense than in the previous century, 21st-century manufacturers will offer products made in automated factories but made to fit each individual customer's needs. Shoppers will be able to choose exactly which options they want from an extensive list of options. The data will be be sent over a computer network to a smart factory that will manufacture and send the product rapidly, whether it is a car or a new pair of shoes.

Self-assembly

Artificial intelligence, as well as more powerful and accurate sensors, are vital keys to developing industrial robots. As robots become easier to use, their cost will drop. By 2025, robots, just like other 21st-century products, will be built in smart factories by other robots.

BLURRED VISION

Many people once feared that robots would rebel against their human masters. Instead, robots have become just one of the many automatic features of the advanced factory.

MICROMACHINES

Machines have been getting smaller and smaller for decades. The arrival of electronic components such as the transistor and integrated circuits have helped shrink many machines to a fraction of their previous size. But miniaturization is not just about shrinking, it is also about packing more functions into the same size unit. Ballpoint pens, for instance, were once used only for writing. Today, some have a clock, radio, and voice recorder built in. The driving forces behind miniaturization have come from the needs of various space programs, the development of new materials and, most importantly, advances in computer technology.

△ Valves used in early electronics were often unreliable. The invention of the transistor in 1947 was a giant step toward the development of micromachinery.

MEMs

MicroElectroMechanical systems, or MEMs for short, are complete machines or components built to the same miniature scale as the circuitry on a silicon chip. Devices from motors and sensing systems the size of a pollen grain to pumps the size of a pinhead could transform engineering in the same way that the silicon chip led to the computer revolution.

▽ Swarms of tiny, cheaply manufactured robot helicopters may be with us by the 2020s. These machines could monitor the condition of crops and get rid of harmful insect pests, without mass spraying of insecticides.

◁ Microengineering has produced many scaled-down devices including this working race car, less than an inch long. The motor that powers the car is only about ¹/₁₀ of an inch in diameter.

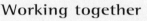

△ These micromachine parts are shown next to a fly's leg for scale. Built using techniques similar to the creation of silicon chips, micromotors and machines could be used extensively in industry by 2025.

Office on an arm

The building blocks are already in place to make portable offices worn as a gauntlet, bracelet, or head-set. Processing and memory components are already small enough to be held in the palm of the hand. One problem that remains is how human and machine will communicate. Miniature keyboards, for example, are difficult to use. Speech recognition is one solution. One day, direct thought control also may be possible.

Working together

Breakthroughs in microengineering and robotics will lead to the rise of many-robot systems. These will consist of robots working together in parallel. These machines will be capable of learning from their collective experience in the same way that bees and termites do. As early as 2010, many-robot systems will be performing a variety of tasks such as minesweeping or land surveying.

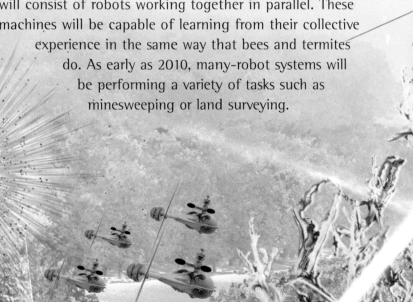

NANOTECHNOLOGY

Nanotechnology is the ultimate in thinking small when it comes to machines. The term comes from the word nanometer, a measurement of one billionth of a meter or the equivalent of about ten atoms long. Nanotechnology is technology and machinery that has been created to this scale. The impact of nanotechnology on almost every area of our lives is potentially limitless. Nanomachines could work within other machines and other objects, maintaining them so that they never break down or wear out. Self-repairing car engines and clothing will reduce waste and usher in a new age. According to one nanotechnology expert, Ralph Merkle, "Nanotechnology can be the cornerstone of future technology, a fundamental factor in the future development of civilization."

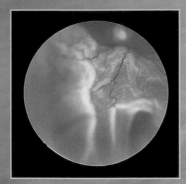

△ A detached retina is an eye condition that can lead to permanent blindness. By 2060, surgery for this condition, as well as many others, will be transformed by nanotechnology.

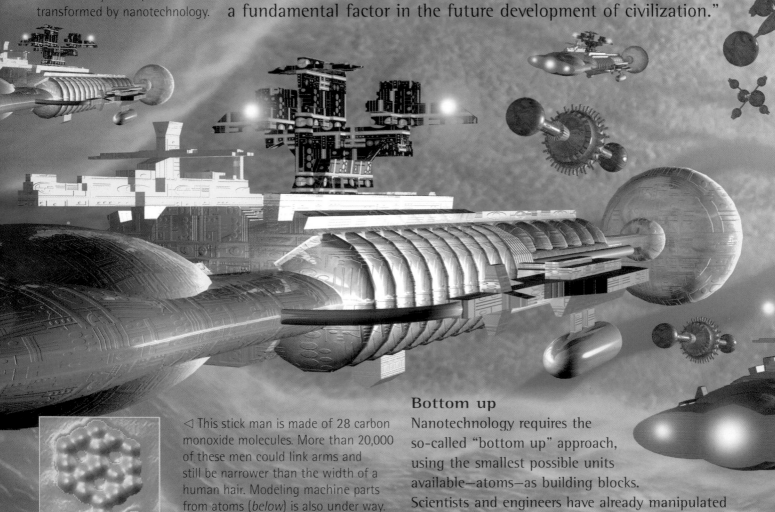

◁ This stick man is made of 28 carbon monoxide molecules. More than 20,000 of these men could link arms and still be narrower than the width of a human hair. Modeling machine parts from atoms (*below*) is also under way.

Bottom up

Nanotechnology requires the so-called "bottom up" approach, using the smallest possible units available—atoms—as building blocks. Scientists and engineers have already manipulated individual atoms and molecules to create patterns and images. By 2010, computer memory will probably use nanotechnology to store vast amounts of data on tiny clusters of atoms and molecules. By 2020, we can expect the first nanomachines to be made.

Saving the planet

Nanotechnology could create paint for road markings
full of very small solar cells that generate pollution-free
electricity from solar power. Smart engines could include
nanomachines that reduce polluting waste compounds.
Fleets of nanorobots, known as nanobots, created in
huge numbers, could work at repairing the ozone
layer or cleaning up areas of the world polluted
by older technology.

Working inside you

One of the most exciting goals of nanotechnology
is the creation of nanomachines that can repair our
bodies from the inside. This would revolutionize our
health. Medical nanobots could enter the bloodstream,
scrubbing our blood vessels free of cholesterol and
unblocking clogged arteries and veins. Smart
toothpaste could contain fleets of nanobots
that detect and remove plaque.

△ At present, oil slicks cause major pollution problems. An army
of nanobots could work at a microscopic level, breaking down
and reprocessing an oil slick before serious damage is done.

◁ Delicate eye surgery may one day be performed by
thousands of nanobots. Working from inside the eye they
will be able to move a detached retina back into position
before repairing it. The larger nanomachines in the foreground
control and supply power to the smaller surgical nanotools.

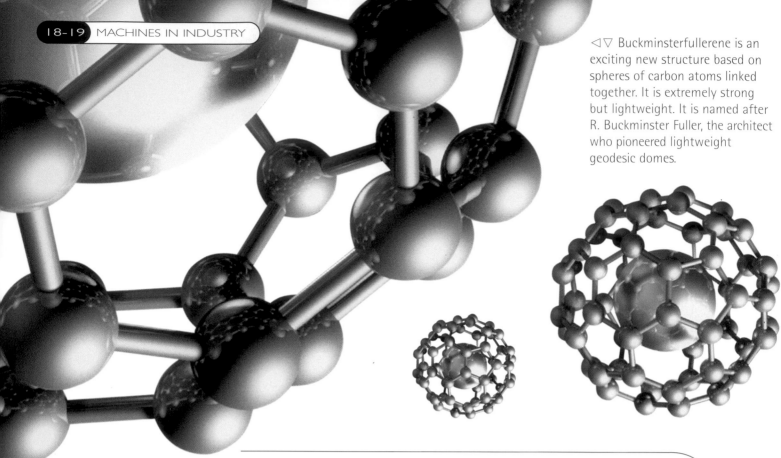

◁▽ Buckminsterfullerene is an exciting new structure based on spheres of carbon atoms linked together. It is extremely strong but lightweight. It is named after R. Buckminster Fuller, the architect who pioneered lightweight geodesic domes.

NEW MATERIALS

Humans have always had the urge to create something new from the raw materials found on Earth. From the discovery of metal alloys created by mixing base metals together in the Bronze Age over 4,000 years ago, to the creation of plastics from oil and petroleum, this drive for new materials has helped shape civilization. In the future we can expect to see many new materials, or developments of old ones. Some of these materials will offer improvements in areas such as strength, heat-resistance, and recyclability. Others will offer radically new and unexpected benefits.

△ Nylon stockings appeared in the early 1940s. They were one of the first products to be developed from processing oil.

Composites

Composite materials are made of several different materials bonded together. Since the early 1970s they have had a huge impact on many machines and products, from personal defense armor to spacecraft. Important composite materials include Kevlar, glass-reinforced plastic (GRP), metal matrix composites, and carbon-reinforced ceramics.

△ Lycra is a fabric that reduces muscle vibration, a major cause of muscle fatigue. This can help athletes to perform better.

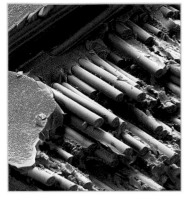

Shape Memory Alloys (SMAs) can remember their original shape and return to it after being stretched or compressed. By the end of the 21st century, homes, offices, and other structures built with SMA materials will be capable of withstanding earthquakes.

△ At 330x magnification, the individual fibers of fiberglass can be seen clearly. Fiberglass is a strong but lightweight composite material.

◁ Glasses made with Shape Memory Alloys have already been produced. They do not break even after being crumpled and crushed.

Electric threads

Smart materials are able to react and adapt to their environment. They are already found in light sensitive sunglasses and "breathable" fabrics. Electrotextiles is one exciting area of development. Researchers have created fibers with carbon in them that can transmit electric signals. Electrotextiles could be used in nerve-stimulating body suits for people with disabilities or in clothes that contain complete communication systems.

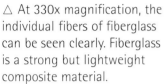

◁ A wide array of electronic devices, from computers and communication systems to health monitoring devices, will be built into the electrotextile clothing of the future.

New materials, new possiblities

Computers, airliners, and many other 20th-century inventions would not have been possible without plastics, new metal alloys, and silicon. New materials in the 21st century will help drive technology in a similar way. Areas that are likely to benefit from advances in materials include superconductivity, nuclear fusion, and virtual reality.

▽ Silica aerogel, developed by NASA, is an almost perfect heat insulator. It is as light as a feather and should have a huge variety of uses from spacecraft to refrigerators.

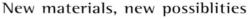

CREATING POWER

Machines have always needed power to work. Until the 1800s, most machines, such as bellows or plows, only required the muscular effort of humans or animals, while a few, such as waterwheels, were driven by the channeling of simple, natural movement. The advent of electricity and the internal combustion engine changed machines forever. Today, power generating plants, oil refineries, and petroleum production sites feed the world's insatiable demand for power. During the 20th century, power consumption increased more than ten times. By the year 2020, world demand for power will have increased again by at least 50 percent. Many of the fuels used today will not last forever. This fact, together with growing environmental concerns, will lead to a greater emphasis on efficient power production, storage, and use. Research into potentially vital areas such as superconductivity, nuclear fusion, and alternative, renewable energies may lead to a major breakthrough that will help us rely less on traditional fuels for power.

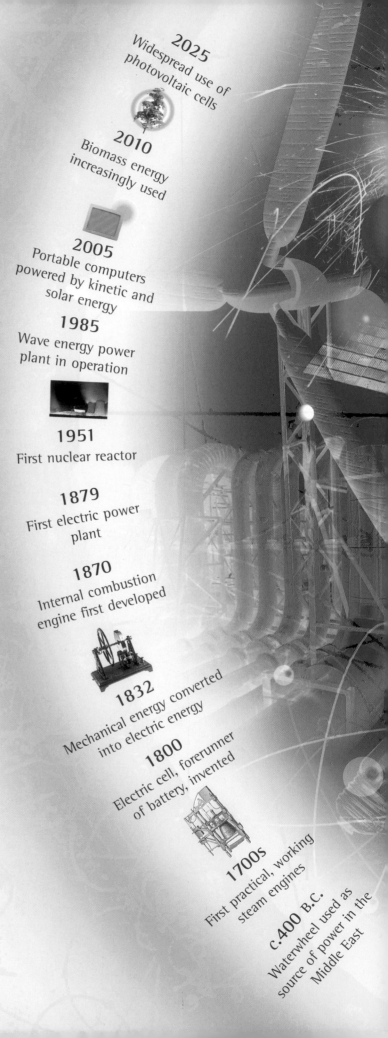

2025
Widespread use of photovoltaic cells

2010
Biomass energy increasingly used

2005
Portable computers powered by kinetic and solar energy

1985
Wave energy power plant in operation

1951
First nuclear reactor

1879
First electric power plant

1870
Internal combustion engine first developed

1832
Mechanical energy converted into electric energy

1800
Electric cell, forerunner of battery, invented

1700s
First practical, working steam engines

c.400 B.C.
Waterwheel used as source of power in the Middle East

FOSSIL FUELS

Coal, oil, and natural gas power the modern world. Formed over millions of years, these fossil fuels are created by layers of earth and rock that have compressed decaying animal and plant matter. During the early decades of the 21st century, humans will continue to rely on these fossil fuels despite the ecological problems created by the air waste gases. Fossil fuels are a finite, nonrenewable resource—they will not last forever at the rate we are using them. Supplies are getting smaller, although not as fast as predicted in the 1960s and 1970s. Since then, new techniques for finding and getting fossil fuels have led to the discovery and recovery of previously unknown supplies.

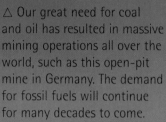

△ Our great need for coal and oil has resulted in massive mining operations all over the world, such as this open-pit mine in Germany. The demand for fossil fuels will continue for many decades to come.

◁ One alternative to gasoline is biofuel, which is made from processing certain plants. Improvements in this process may lead to much more widespread use of biofuel.

△ Connah's Quay gas-fired power plant in North Wales, U.K. uses an advanced system called combined cycle gas turbine (CCGT). It is 40 percent more efficient than a regular coal-fired station.

Remote operation

Even with advances in solar power and other alternative energies, fossil fuels will still be needed both as a fuel and as a raw material for plastics and other substances. The search for new supplies, from 2015 onward, will be done by a new generation of robots and intelligent machines. By 2030, remote ocean mining and drilling will take place in many parts of the world. Drilling rigs and coal mines will also be operated remotely in areas, such as deserts, that are difficult to live in.

Nightmare scenario

The dwindling of fossil fuels will have a major impact on the planet. We are dependent on machines—many of which rely on fossil fuels to make them work. No power means no machines, and society would grind to a halt. Even a major increase in fuel prices could lead to a catastrophic world recession because the economy is directly linked to the price of fossil fuels. The search for alternative energy sources will become more and more important during the 21st century.

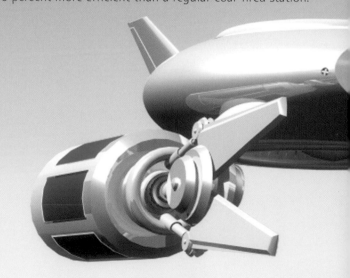

More efficiency

With the world demand for electricity expected to double by 2020, there will be major efforts to make more efficient use of fossil fuels in the 21st century. One way to achieve this is to improve the way we store electricity and transmit it. Maintaining power lines will become vital, and by 2015, we can expect to see special power line robots working more quickly, safely, and efficiently than humans can.

◁ Core samples taken from the arctic wastelands, or tundra, indicate that there are large oil and gas deposits. By 2025, remote automated drilling platforms may be built there. They will require only rare maintenance visits from human personnel.

The search for fuels and other resources may eventually lead to exploration and mining of bodies other than the Earth. By 2100, mining units might recover ore from the moon and asteroids. The ore will be reprocessed into high-grade fuel and then transported back to Earth.

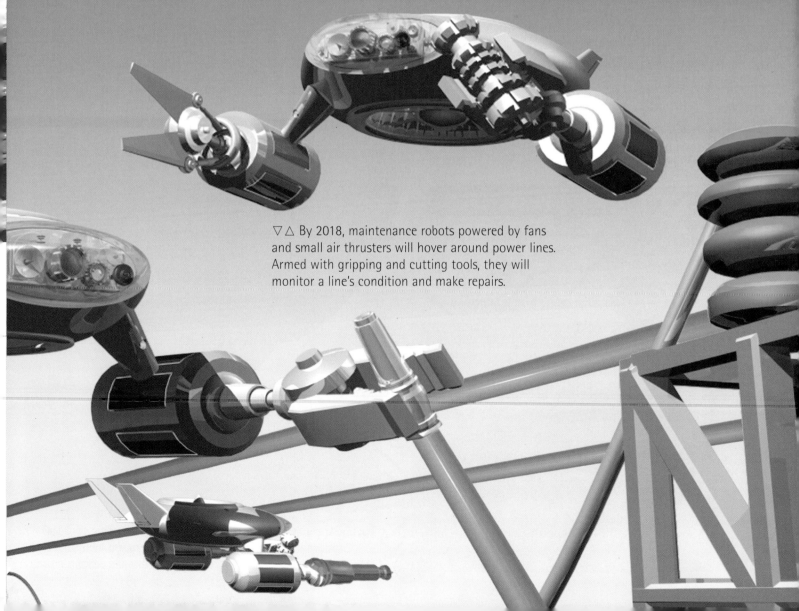

▽△ By 2018, maintenance robots powered by fans and small air thrusters will hover around power lines. Armed with gripping and cutting tools, they will monitor a line's condition and make repairs.

ENERGY FROM THE CORES

Nuclear fusion—the process behind the sun's awesome power—has provided the Earth with energy for billions of years. However, the fraction of the sun's output that reaches Earth is a staggering 30,000 times more than the energy we actually use. This incredible resource will give us sustainable, pollution-free power if scientists can learn how to use it more efficiently. Although it is small in comparison to the sun's energy, the Earth's core also generates considerable heat. Work continues on geothermal technologies that will harness some of this heat energy and convert it into electrical power. In the future, it is likely to increase in importance as an additional pollution-free energy supply.

△ The technology behind solar power is not new. This solar cooker, which boils the water in a coffee pot, dates back to the 1960s.

△ Solar-powered calculators have been available since the 1970s. They use photovoltaic cells to convert sunlight into electrical power.

Solar heat

One form of solar power generation makes use of the sun's warming energy. It uses solar heat reflectors to gather the sun's heat and focus it on a collector. Heat collectors work like radiators in reverse—they collect heat that is used to boil a liquid such as oil or water. In the case of water, the steam that is created drives electricity-generating turbines.

△ This solar reflector in the Pyrenees in France is made up of 9,500 mirrors and automatically turns to follow the sun.

Sunlight power

Light energy from the sun can also generate solar power. Photovoltaic cells consist of two layers. When the light strikes the top layer of cells, it knocks electrons free from their atoms. These electrons move between the two layers, helping to generate an electric current. As photovoltaic cells become more efficient and cheaper to manufacture, a boom in solar power is likely to occur. In the coming years, photovoltaic cells will appear on cars, buildings, and even clothing, where they could power lightweight electronic devices.

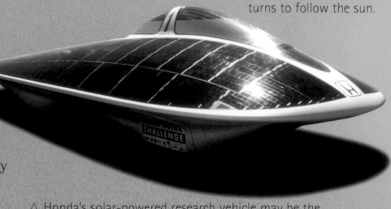

△ Honda's solar-powered research vehicle may be the forerunner of solar vehicles found on the road by the 2020s.

More efficiency

With the world demand for electricity expected to double by 2020, there will be major efforts to make more efficient use of fossil fuels in the 21st century. One way to achieve this is to improve the way we store electricity and transmit it. Maintaining power lines will become vital, and by 2015, we can expect to see special power line robots working more quickly, safely, and efficiently than humans can.

◁ Core samples taken from the arctic wastelands, or tundra, indicate that there are large oil and gas deposits. By 2025, remote automated drilling platforms may be built there. They will require only rare maintenance visits from human personnel.

The search for fuels and other resources may eventually lead to exploration and mining of bodies other than the Earth. By 2100, mining units might recover ore from the moon and asteroids. The ore will be reprocessed into high-grade fuel and then transported back to Earth.

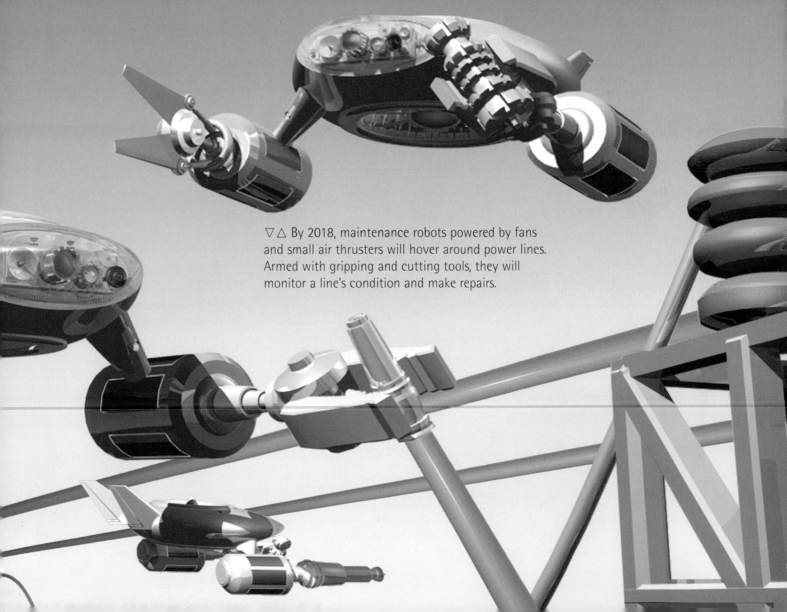

▽△ By 2018, maintenance robots powered by fans and small air thrusters will hover around power lines. Armed with gripping and cutting tools, they will monitor a line's condition and make repairs.

ENERGY FROM ATOMS

△ Calder Hall was the first nuclear power plant in the U.K. It began generating electricity in 1956 and is still in use today.

Nuclear fission—the process of splitting atoms—generates previously unimagined amounts of power without using up fossil fuel supplies. However, nuclear power does have serious disadvantages. The high levels of radioactivity generated pose a potentially lethal health risk. There are also enormous costs involved in safeguarding against such risks and dealing with radioactive waste. Nuclear power development is slow at present but, if fossil fuel supplies dwindle and global warming fears increase, it is possible that the 21st century will see nuclear power play an important role as a power resource.

Public image

Nuclear power produces few of the polluting gases that cause acid rain or global warming. However, unlike other technologies in the 21st century, nuclear power will have to overcome negative public opinion. Confidence in nuclear power took a sharp downturn after incidents such as the 1986 Chernobyl disaster in the Ukraine, and the continuing concerns over waste disposal. Scientists will continue to work to reduce risks and develop safer nuclear power.

△ Tokamaks are research reactors that generate the extreme temperatures needed for nuclear fusion. They use a doughnut-shaped arrangement of powerful electromagnets, along with high-energy particle beams.

◁ In nuclear fission, a neutron collides with an unstable U-235 atom, causing it to split. This releases more neutrons and a great deal of energy. With more U-235 atoms present, this sets off a chain reaction.

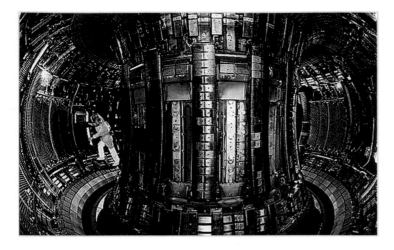

△ This tokamak fusion reactor is part of the Joint European Torus project in the U.K. Other research establishments use lasers to generate the necessary heat.

Waste disposal

The disposal of the high-level radioactive waste created by the nuclear power process is a huge problem. The waste has to be stored for as long as 10,000 years before its radioactivity drops to harmless levels. Most of the world's nuclear waste is in temporary storage facilities awaiting a decision on its fate. By 2010, permanent facilities for long-term storage will have to be built despite the fierce public debate that may arise when it comes to finding a place for them.

▷ Vitrification fixes radioactive waste in an inert glass or ceramic compound. It is then encased in a heavy, metal cannister prior to being buried underground.

The holy grail

In the process of nuclear fusion, heavy hydrogen atoms join together to form helium in a self-sustaining reaction that produces enormous amounts of energy. However, this only occurs at temperatures of millions of degrees Fahrenheit. Scientists are developing different ways of heating atoms to these levels and building a container that can safely handle such temperatures. Whether the goal of safe and unlimited commercial nuclear fusion is a possibility is a question that is not likely to be answered until the middle of the 21st century.

BLURRED VISION

In the 1930s, nuclear power promised a golden age of cheap, clean, limitless energy. By the mid-1950s, when nuclear power plants were first built, long-term waste storage and fears of contamination were major issues.

△ Fast breeder reactors, like Dounreay in Scotland, can produce up to 60 times the energy of a regular nuclear fission reactor. However, there are still technological problems and high costs.

ENERGY FROM THE CORES

Nuclear fusion—the process behind the sun's awesome power—has provided the Earth with energy for billions of years. However, the fraction of the sun's output that reaches Earth is a staggering 30,000 times more than the energy we actually use. This incredible resource will give us sustainable, pollution-free power if scientists can learn how to use it more efficiently. Although it is small in comparison to the sun's energy, the Earth's core also generates considerable heat. Work continues on geothermal technologies that will harness some of this heat energy and convert it into electrical power. In the future, it is likely to increase in importance as an additional pollution-free energy supply.

△ The technology behind solar power is not new. This solar cooker, which boils the water in a coffee pot, dates back to the 1960s.

△ Solar-powered calculators have been available since the 1970s. They use photovoltaic cells to convert sunlight into electrical power.

Solar heat

One form of solar power generation makes use of the sun's warming energy. It uses solar heat reflectors to gather the sun's heat and focus it on a collector. Heat collectors work like radiators in reverse—they collect heat that is used to boil a liquid such as oil or water. In the case of water, the steam that is created drives electricity-generating turbines.

△ This solar reflector in the Pyrenees in France is made up of 9,500 mirrors and automatically turns to follow the sun.

Sunlight power

Light energy from the sun can also generate solar power. Photovoltaic cells consist of two layers. When the light strikes the top layer of cells, it knocks electrons free from their atoms. These electrons move between the two layers, helping to generate an electric current. As photovoltaic cells become more efficient and cheaper to manufacture, a boom in solar power is likely to occur. In the coming years, photovoltaic cells will appear on cars, buildings, and even clothing, where they could power lightweight electronic devices.

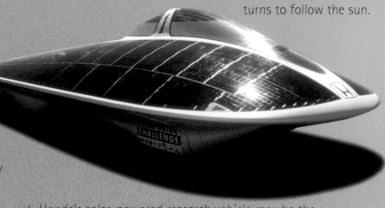

△ Honda's solar-powered research vehicle may be the forerunner of solar vehicles found on the road by the 2020s.

Hot rocks

Geothermal power uses energy from under the Earth's surface to heat water. This water is either used to supply heating and hot water to nearby homes and factories, or it is pumped through a heat exchanger. This converts it into steam that is used to drive electricity generators. From 2020 onward, geothermal power plants will become more common, as breakthroughs in drilling deeper into the Earth and the use of Hot Dry Rock (HDR) technology make it possible to build geothermal plants in many more locations.

△ Icelandic bathers enjoy the hot water generated by a geothermal power plant. These power plants are located in areas of intense thermal activity.

△ Future geothermal power plants may be completely automatic and sited in areas of great thermal, or even volcanic, activity. They will be remote controlled from a distance by human technicians. Maintenance robots and machines will monitor and make routine repairs.

▽ Each panel of this solar power plant consists of thousands of solar cells and a grid of metal conductors that turn sunlight into an electrical current.

◁ The first battery was invented in 1800 by the Italian scientist Alessandro Volta and called a voltaic pile. It consisted of discs of copper, zinc, and cardboard saturated with a salt solution.

▽ A technique called computational fluid dynamics (CFD) allows computers to check on the effects of gases and liquids around an object such as this space plane. CFD helps scientists cut down friction and other energy waste.

GREATER EFFICIENCY

Once a machine is invented, people have usually tried to improve its efficiency—to make it do more with less power. This will become even more vital in the future—especially with growing worries about the effects of some kinds of power on the environment. Scientists and engineers are researching new ways of getting more with less by improving design, streamlining, and using advanced materials. Greater efficiency is a goal for all future machines—not just the electronic and mechanical machines and the vehicles that consume power, but also the power plants and transmission devices that generate power in the first place.

◁ A combination of lightweight materials and a streamlined design are behind the incredible performance of this record-breaking race bike.

Hot rocks

Geothermal power uses energy from under the Earth's surface to heat water. This water is either used to supply heating and hot water to nearby homes and factories, or it is pumped through a heat exchanger. This converts it into steam that is used to drive electricity generators. From 2020 onward, geothermal power plants will become more common, as breakthroughs in drilling deeper into the Earth and the use of Hot Dry Rock (HDR) technology make it possible to build geothermal plants in many more locations.

△ Icelandic bathers enjoy the hot water generated by a geothermal power plant. These power plants are located in areas of intense thermal activity.

△ Future geothermal power plants may be completely automatic and sited in areas of great thermal, or even volcanic, activity. They will be remote controlled from a distance by human technicians. Maintenance robots and machines will monitor and make routine repairs.

▽ Each panel of this solar power plant consists of thousands of solar cells and a grid of metal conductors that turn sunlight into an electrical current.

HARNESSING THE ELEMENTS

△ The mechanical power created by waterwheels has been used for centuries to grind corn and pump water.

Fears that fossil fuel supplies were running low and concerns about the damage caused by their emissions led to much research in the late 20th century on alternative, low-pollution forms of power. Nature provides us with potential energy sources that are endless even if they are not constant. The movement of wind, waves, and tides can all be turned into useful energy. In the 21st century, scientists and engineers will work on creating efficient, cost-effective energy generation from wind and water. A major breakthrough will make a huge difference in the way future generations obtain power.

△ The first tidal power plant was built in France across the Rance River. It has been in operation since 1966.

Water power

Hydroelectric power (HEP) uses the force of water flowing downward to move turbines that generate electricity. Different types of turbine are used for different geographical locations. The largest current scheme is at Itaipu on the Brazil–Paraguay border, and it generates 10,000 megawatts of power. Research into new, more efficient types of turbines will result in a number of hydroelectric projects across the globe exceeding this power-generating figure by 2015.

▽ Offshore wind farms could be a feature of many coastlines in the future. Denmark is leading the way. By 2030, it is estimated that more than 25 percent of all Denmark's electricity will be generated by offshore wind farms.

△ Mountainous locations and large dams, such as the Hoover Dam in Arizona, provide a fast-flowing water source needed to make a hydroelectric project effective.

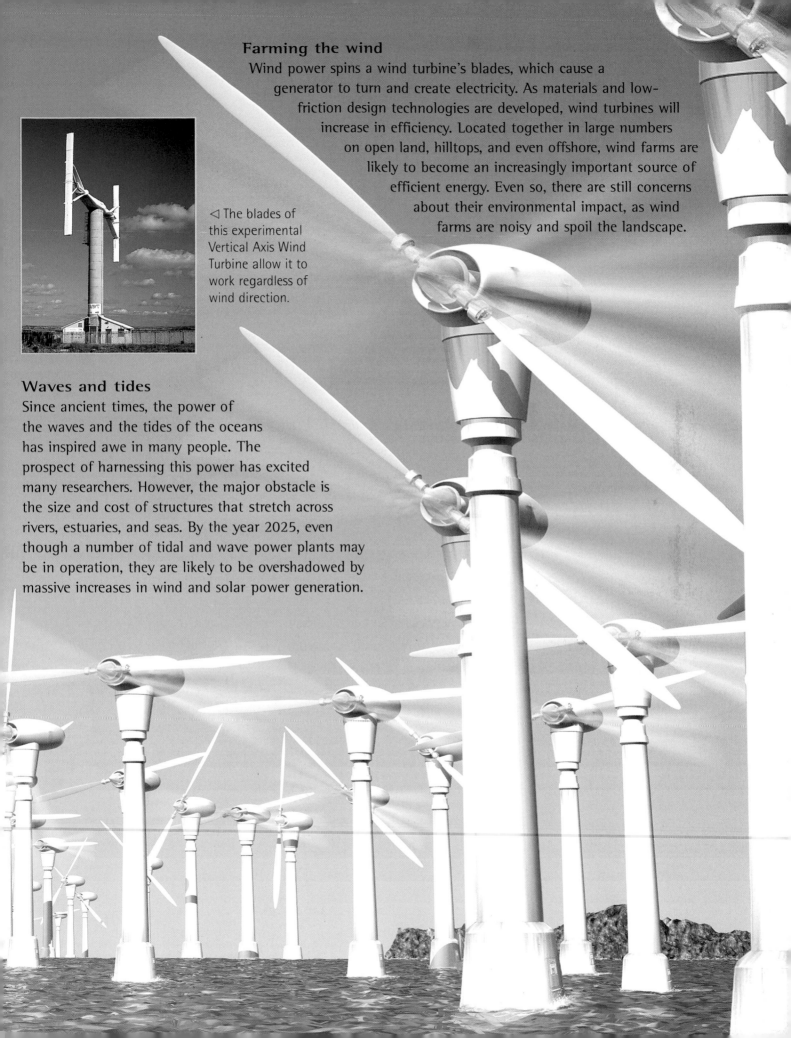

Farming the wind

Wind power spins a wind turbine's blades, which cause a generator to turn and create electricity. As materials and low-friction design technologies are developed, wind turbines will increase in efficiency. Located together in large numbers on open land, hilltops, and even offshore, wind farms are likely to become an increasingly important source of efficient energy. Even so, there are still concerns about their environmental impact, as wind farms are noisy and spoil the landscape.

◁ The blades of this experimental Vertical Axis Wind Turbine allow it to work regardless of wind direction.

Waves and tides

Since ancient times, the power of the waves and the tides of the oceans has inspired awe in many people. The prospect of harnessing this power has excited many researchers. However, the major obstacle is the size and cost of structures that stretch across rivers, estuaries, and seas. By the year 2025, even though a number of tidal and wave power plants may be in operation, they are likely to be overshadowed by massive increases in wind and solar power generation.

◁ The first battery was invented in 1800 by the Italian scientist Alessandro Volta and called a voltaic pile. It consisted of discs of copper, zinc, and cardboard saturated with a salt solution.

▽ A technique called computational fluid dynamics (CFD) allows computers to check on the effects of gases and liquids around an object such as this space plane. CFD helps scientists cut down friction and other energy waste.

GREATER EFFICIENCY

Once a machine is invented, people have usually tried to improve its efficiency—to make it do more with less power. This will become even more vital in the future—especially with growing worries about the effects of some kinds of power on the environment. Scientists and engineers are researching new ways of getting more with less by improving design, streamlining, and using advanced materials. Greater efficiency is a goal for all future machines—not just the electronic and mechanical machines and the vehicles that consume power, but also the power plants and transmission devices that generate power in the first place.

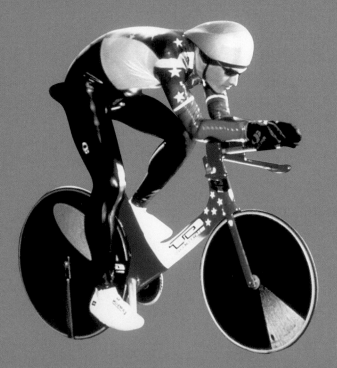

◁ A combination of lightweight materials and a streamlined design are behind the incredible performance of this record-breaking race bike.

Electric power

Power plants in the early 21st century will be able to produce electricity with less fuel than we use now. At the same time, improved technology will transmit the electricity to homes, offices, and factories more efficiently. Batteries are also likely to improve. The superbatteries of the 2020s will store far more electricity than today's. Many more batteries will be rechargeable and easier to recycle.

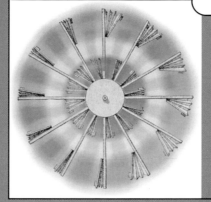

The idea of a perpetual motion machine, which makes enough power, once you start it, to keep itself running forever, has occupied many scientists over the centuries. It is now believed that such a machine goes against the laws of physics.

▷ The Japanese Magnetic Levitation (Maglev) train uses powerful electric magnets to raise the train just above the track. The huge reduction in friction results in a faster, more efficient train.

Electricity without energy loss

The ability of certain materials to conduct electricity at incredibly low temperatures with no resistance or power loss is called superconductivity. A lot of research is still needed to develop superconducting materials that are practical to shape and use, and that work at less extreme temperatures. By 2030, we should begin to see superconductors in extremely efficient electric motors and in power lines that can transmit electricity for hundreds of miles without energy loss.

A lack of friction

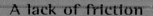

Friction—the resistance caused by two things rubbing together—creates wear and heat, and reduces the performance of many machines. Research into ways of minimizing friction will continue into the 21st century. Lubrication systems should improve, computer models will help improve steamlining, and new materials will be created that produce very little friction.

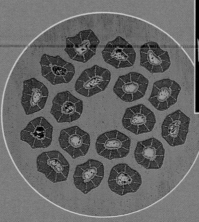

◁△ YBCO is a ceramic superconductor that works at relatively high temperatures. It allows electricity to be conducted without resistance.

MILITARY MACHINES

Conflict and warfare have always been a feature of human societies. Sticks and stones were some of the earliest weapons. Gradually, methods were developed to propel weapons across greater distances and with more force, from the slingshot and crossbow to cannons, firearms, and torpedoes. Advances in weapon development reached a new stage in the 20th century when the human race had the capability to destroy life on the planet many times over. With this terrifying ability came a new responsibility to prevent a third World War from occurring. Conflict will still exist, however, in the 21st century. Terrorism and localized warfare will continue as various groups fight for control within small areas of land. In this complex future world, where enemies are harder to locate, the need for up-to-the-minute information will increase, as will rapid strike forces and unmanned, autonomous weapons and systems.

1945 Atomic bomb detonated

1944 First jet aircraft flown in combat

1916 Tanks first used in World War I

1911 First military aircraft used for reconnaissance

1864 First self-propelled torpedo

1835 First revolver

1300s Cannons used in warfare

A.D. 600s Gunpowder invented

2030
Antisatellite weapons launched

2025
Explosive robots used in sabotage operations

1983
Stealth fighters and bombers in service

SPYING AND DEFENSE

Ever since wars began, opposing sides have attempted to find out as much as they can about the enemy's position, size, and weaponry. Spying has always involved sending human scouts and agents behind enemy lines. However, the future is likely to see unmanned machines taking over, with human operatives safely conducting surveillance operations from a distance using computer networks. Advances in information technology will mean that a person's actions on the Internet and other networks can be easily traced. By 2010, electronic tagging by minitransmitters may also allow people to be tracked accurately without their knowledge.

△▽ Cameras have long been used for spying, often hidden in household items or miniaturized to make them harder to detect. Advances in microengineering will continue to shrink the size of radios, bugs, and cameras—the tools of the spy's trade.

Stealth

"See but not be seen" is a motto for all spies and especially for the pilots of spy and reconnaissance aircraft that fly over enemy territory. Stealth technology is designed to confuse enemy radar and other sensors and allow aircraft to fly undetected. Featuring radar-absorbing paints, angled facets, and low-heat emitting engines, this technology is being improved for the second generation of stealth planes and is also being adapted to land and sea vehicles.

△ Spy movies like the James Bond series tend to show agents that operate alone. In reality, many spies work in close contact with their controllers.

△▷ The minimum size of an object seen from a spy satellite is known as its resolution. Current satellites are believed to have a resolution of about 20 inches. Future models will be able to read over a person's shoulder, if they are not already capable of doing so.

Spies in the sky

Despite the effectiveness of stealth technology, pilots and crew will continue to be at risk. One viable alternative is automated, computer-controlled pilotless aircraft. Pilotless drones have already been used for some routine duties, but as computer control becomes more sophisticated, unmanned aerial vehicles (UAVs) will fly more and more missions over enemy territory. By 2015, many reconnaissance and spying flights will be performed by UAVs.

Spying from space

It is no secret that many of the satellites orbiting Earth are used for spying. What is secret, however, is the definition and quality of the images. The results that the public sees are probably not the very best that intelligence agencies can obtain. Satellites are used because they provide relatively risk-free information gathering. However, this may not always be the case. NASA and the Pentagon are currently spending $50 million a year on developing antispy satellite devices.

▷ The Lockheed *B2* bomber has a stealth flying wing design covered in radar-absorbing material. This allows it to fly deep into enemy territory without detection.

◁ Everything a spy needs to conduct video surveillance can be contained in a briefcase. Remote-operated machines may perform this sort of surveillance task by 2020.

PERSONAL WEAPONS

Until the discovery of gunpowder in the 10th century, most personal weapons, such as spears and swords, relied on human muscle power. With the application of gunpowder people began to use artificially-powered weapons such as cannons, muskets, and later, machine guns and revolvers. These worked over far greater distances than earlier weapons and were much more deadly. In the first half of the 21st century, firearms will be similar to those of the late 20th century. The main differences will be in how the new weapons are targeted and the ways in which people can be protected from their destructive effects.

△ Rapid-fire machine guns such as the *Maxim Mk1*, designed in 1884, completely changed the nature of warfare.

Invention then protection

Weapon development goes through a cycle of invention then protection. As soon as a weapon is created, efforts are made to protect against it. By 2010, when even the smallest handgun will pack a lethal punch, more effective and lightweight body armor will be developed that uses blends of new composites and other materials. By 2030, some armor may offer stealth capablilities or provide power in the form of solar cells built into the outer shell.

△ This body armor, constructed out of woven meshes of steel and composites, such as Kevlar, can withstand a bullet fired even at short range.

▷ Members of the French Special Police Force are equipped with body armor and image-intensifying goggles.

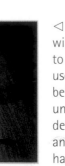

◁ By 2015, many guns will use microprocessors to detect a permitted user's electronic signature before the safety catch is unlocked. Alternative safety devices may scan the palm and fingerprints of the hand holding the weapon.

Battles without bullets

Lethal personal weapons that do not use bullets may be a very real threat by 2020. These weapons will use concentrated toxic gas sprays, light beams, or sound focused at a high frequency to inflict harm. Many major military powers are already researching ways to protect against such possible threats. The threat of chemical and biological warfare is also likely to remain, and efforts will be focused on developing fail-safe methods of detection as well as effective antidotes.

△ The *S.I.G.* assault rifle is equipped with an advanced sighting mechanism that uses a laser for pinpoint accuracy.

◁ The sticky stunner projectile administers an electric shock that stuns and temporarily disables the target.

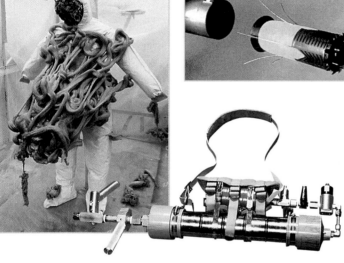

△ The sticky foam gun fires large quantities of very adhesive foam that stops a target from moving or reaching for a weapon.

Nonlethal weaponry

By 2015, many security and police forces will be equipped with effective nondeadly weapons that stun or temporarily disable a target. Weapons being developed include sticky foam guns and sticky stunners. Sticky foam guns fire a mass of disabling adhesive foam to prevent someone from escaping. Sticky stunners fire a soft-barbed or glue-covered object. When they hit a target they temporarily disable the person with an electric shock.

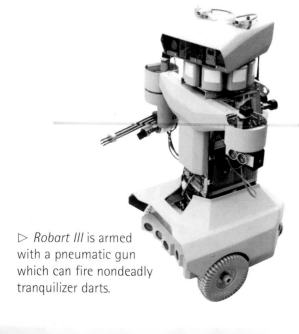

▷ *Robart III* is armed with a pneumatic gun which can fire nondeadly tranquilizer darts.

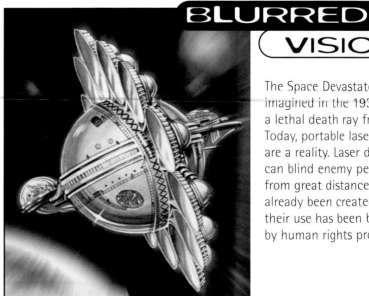

BLURRED VISION

The Space Devastator, as imagined in the 1930s, fired a lethal death ray from space. Today, portable laser weapons are a reality. Laser dazers which can blind enemy personnel from great distances have already been created but their use has been banned by human rights protocols.

◁ The Joint Strike Fighter, in service from 2012, will be a high-performance, multirole fighter with stealth technology. It will have the ability to climb over a mile in ten seconds.

Delivery systems are the part of a military force that delivers weapons to their target. Tanks, aircraft, battleships, and submarines were all potent delivery systems in the late 20th century.

DELIVERY SYSTEMS

Some methods of attack, such as rapid air strikes, will increase in importance throughout the 21st century while the role of others, such as bomber aircraft and battleships, will diminish. Unmanned delivery systems are likely to overtake traditional systems by the middle of the 21st century.

△ The aircraft of Baron von Richtofen's so-called "flying circus" were a formidable force in World War I. Combat, or dogfights, between enemy aircraft took place at very close range.

▷ These single mission robot insects, no bigger than a compact disc, will be dropped from the air or launched from land vehicles. Cheap to produce, they can be sent out in large numbers and carry small but highly concentrated explosive charges.

Downsizing

Flagship forces such as unwieldy battle cruisers, massed land battalions, and aircraft carriers will probably continue to be used by the major powers for their deterrent effect. However, the role of striking at enemy targets will probably be taken over by swifter, smaller, and more accurate delivery systems in the air and on and under the water. Many of these systems will be equipped with stealth technology to avoid detection.

Missiles and smart bombs

The power of unmanned delivery systems has been recognized ever since the German V1 and V2 rockets were used during World War II. In the 21st century, we can expect to see unmanned air machines such as fighters and bombers in action, as well as "smarter" missiles. These unmanned airborne delivery systems will be able to perform maneuvers, reach targets, and take risks that are too dangerous for humans.

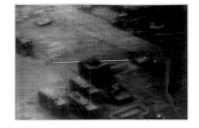

△ Smart bombs with on-board navigation sensors were used to deadly effect by the Allied forces in the Persian Gulf War.

△ Stealth technology is being developed for land and sea machines to make them almost undetectable by enemy radar.

Access all areas

Unmanned delivery systems will not be restricted to airborne devices. Robotic delivery systems will also be developed that work under water and on all kinds of landscape. By 2025, we will probably see relatively cheap robot bombs being used, based on an insect design. These will be ideal for scuttling over difficult ground before detonating when they reach their target.

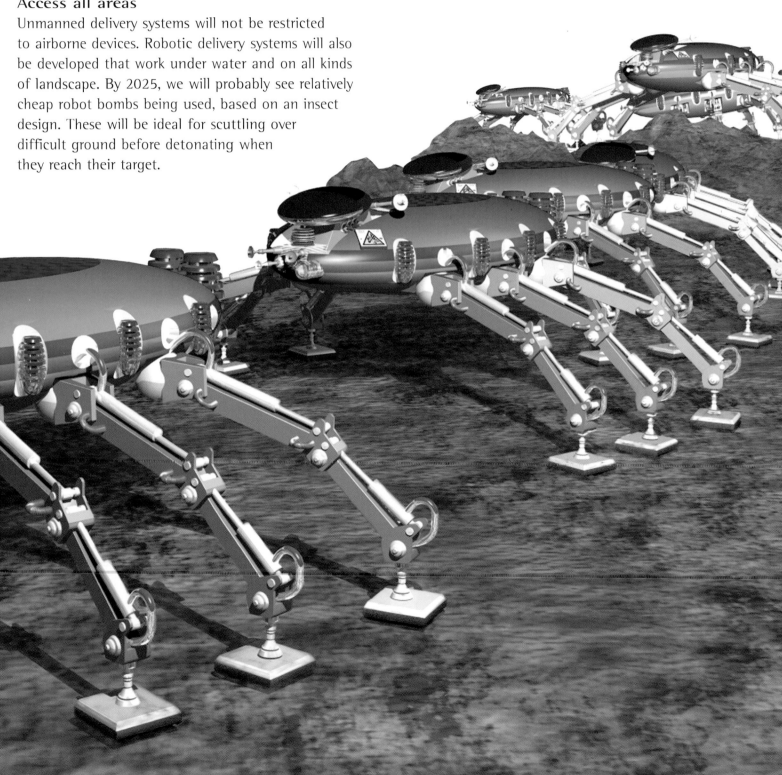

FUTURE BATTLEGROUNDS

Until World War II, most major conflicts involved lines of infantry, cavalry, or motor vehicles moving slowly and painfully forward to engage in battle. The success of the highly mobile *Blitzkreig* ("Lightning War") in the early stages of World War II, transformed the slow-moving nature of battles forever. Military conflicts of the future are likely to be small-scale and fought in small areas. They will call on a military force's advanced communications systems as well as its capability to get machines and personnel to the conflict zone as quickly and secretly as possible.

△ Trench warfare was a feature of World War I. Many lives were lost because of constant bombardment and disease.

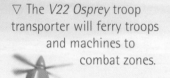

▽ The *V22 Osprey* troop transporter will ferry troops and machines to combat zones.

Rapid response

Small-scale, unexpected, and fast-changing conflicts mean the military forces of tomorrow will need to be highly mobile and capable of gathering in hours rather than weeks. Future conflicts will see a machine-led approach with unmanned scout vehicles and tilt-rotor aircraft that can hover to load and unload troops.

△ Command centers in the 21st century will rely on advanced communications systems to control forces.

Elite forces

By 2020, the most advanced military powers will be phasing out big battalions of troops in favor of two distinct types of soldier—peacekeeping forces who work alongside, or instead of, the police to quell civil unrest; and highly-trained elite forces. Elite forces will be small in number and very mobile. They will have two-way communication with command centers from where the tactical and organizational war will be fought.

Smart fighters

Elite troops will be equipped to operate alone or in small groups. In addition to two-way radio and data links, they will also be equipped with body-monitoring equipment and night vision goggles. Smart uniforms will have body armor and may have the ability to change camouflage pattern to fit the surroundings.

△ The latest battlewear already incorporates bulletproof visors. Future visors will feature displays that tell the soldier what to do and how the battle is going.

△ Night vision goggles will become standard equipment for elite troops of the future.

▽ By 2030, elite troops will be working with robot infantry. Tiny sensors, dropped on the battlefield, will send back vital information to the command center.

2040 Space hotels in operation

2012 Fully automated stores with robot assistants

MACHINES
NEAR AND FAR

Many machines, from the winch used at a water well to weapons such as the cannon, were designed to extend the range of a person's actions. This trend continued throughout the 20th century but with one important advance—machines were created that could also be operated by remote control, particularly in dangerous places such as nuclear power plants. Sophisticated communications and control systems allow teleoperated machines to be controlled by people who are a great distance away. Automation is another important development. Automatic machines and robots with basic intelligence are taking over many day-to-day tasks that were once performed by humans. Automated machines are also working far from home, exploring space and the planets in our solar system.

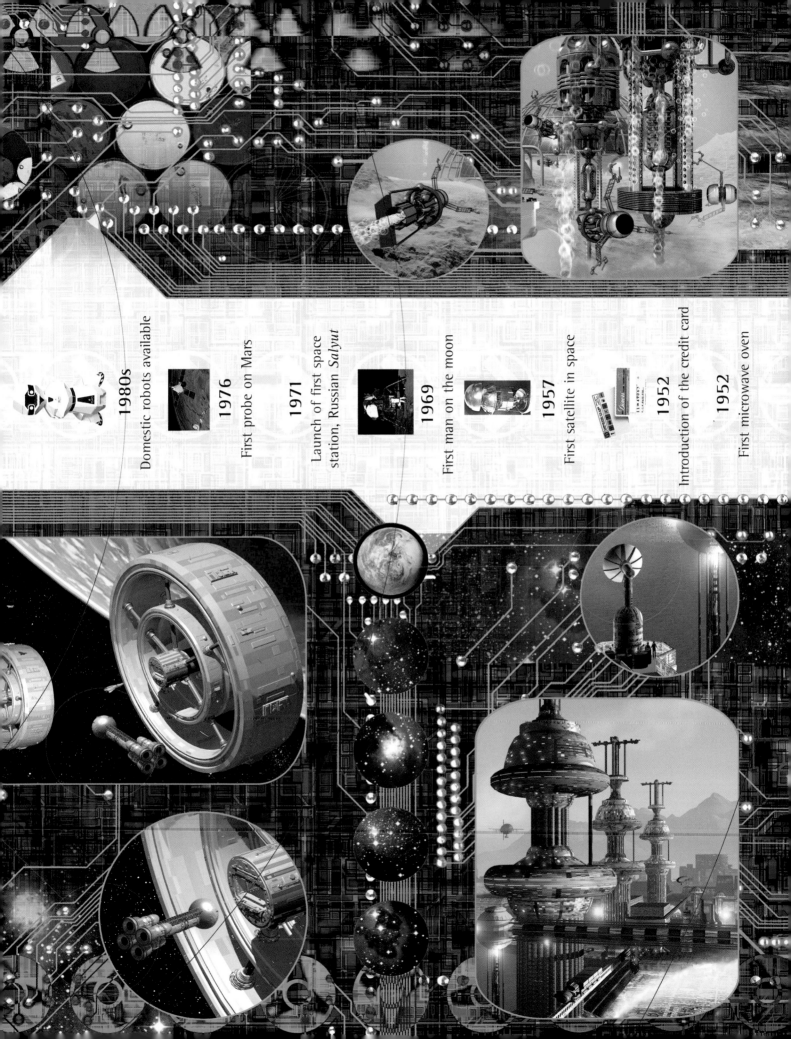

1980s
Domestic robots available

1976
First probe on Mars

1971
Launch of first space station, Russian *Salyut*

1969
First man on the moon

1957
First satellite in space

1952
Introduction of the credit card

1952
First microwave oven

IN THE HOME

△ The microwave oven, which cuts down the cooking time of many foods, was hailed as the ultimate in labor-saving devices when it was first launched in the 1950s.

During the 20th century, many machines, from washing machines to food processors, were designed to cut down the time spent on household chores. New machines in future homes will work even harder for us. As the cost of microprocessors continues to drop, more and more homes will be controlled by computer networks and a fully programmable series of intelligent electronic functions. These will be built into the house as it is constructed and will include full security systems, climate and environmental control, and advanced telecommunications features.

No cord accord

Wireless power networks will be found in many high-tech homes built after 2015. Most of the electricity required by the network will come from conventional sources, but some will be generated by a home's own solar panels. Many electrical devices, from irons to televisions, will be powered by advanced, superefficient batteries, allowing cordless operation. Electrical outlets will be replaced by recharging stations for these batteries.

Faster food

Advances in food technology and genetic engineering of fresh foods will make washing, cutting, and peeling a thing of the past. Kitchens will eventually be little more than a place where food can be stored, heated, and served. Even so, pots, pans, and chopping boards will not disappear completely. Some people will still prefer to keep the human touch when cooking food.

△ Intelligent kitchens, such as this research model in Seattle, will be standard in homes from 2020. They will feature smart stoves that scan cooking data imprinted on food and apply the correct amount of heat for the right amount of time.

◁ The intelligent garbage can uses magnets and material sensors to sort different types of garbage for recycling.

CRYSTAL BALL

By 2040, conventional carpet cleaning—either by robots or humans—may be a thing of the past. Electronically controlled carpet fibers could move dust and dirt to the edge of the carpet where it would be collected in easy-to-empty containers.

△ By 2020, pans made from smart metal alloys will be able to sense and adjust exactly how much heat they conduct. This will help them prevent, for example, water or a sauce from boiling over.

Environmental control

Many machines installed in the houses of the future will monitor and adjust different aspects of the environment. Energy conservation will continue to be an important issue. To ensure efficiency, intelligent heating monitors will be found around the house. These will automatically adjust temperatures and be linked to electromechanical devices that open and shut windows and doors in order to reduce the energy used in heating or cooling.

▽▷ Smart glass will be able to measure the amount and intensity of light passing through it and automatically dim the glass if the light is too bright.

DOMESTIC ROBOTS

△ This robot lawn mower is solar-powered and has simple crash detectors and sensors that keep the mower within its programmed area.

△ Voice-activated toy robots are the starting point for educational robots for young children. Robot teachers will appear in homes from around 2010 onward.

It is estimated that by 2015, there will be at least three million robots working in industry. Besides factories, robots will also be used in places such as supermarkets, as security guards, and in hospitals, as carers and helpers. By 2025, office robots and automatic machines will be handling many basic tasks now performed by people, for example, inputting data and handling phone calls. A new generation of home robots will also be developed. Unlike the novelty toy robots of the 1990s, or the one-function machines of 2000–2010, these will be truly versatile robots capable of performing a wide variety of tasks.

Home help

Some domestic robots are likely to be used as carers for the old, the sick, and the disabled. Robot carers, unlike humans, will not need to take time off for their own lives and will be able to offer 24-hour care and assistance. They will constantly check a home patient's medical condition and send back data over a computer network to doctors in a hospital or medical office.

Early learning

Robotic home teachers will provide one-to-one instruction for many young children in the future. Using artificial intelligence, these robots will perform a range of tasks and activities. Robot teachers will help children acquire early learning skills from basic shape and color recognition to counting, reading, and writing.

▷ The robot assistant of 2030 will have a lightweight robot arm for some physical chores. Most of its work, however, will be done over computer networks. It will communicate directly with these networks using a probe that fits into a special wall socket or by using wireless communications systems.

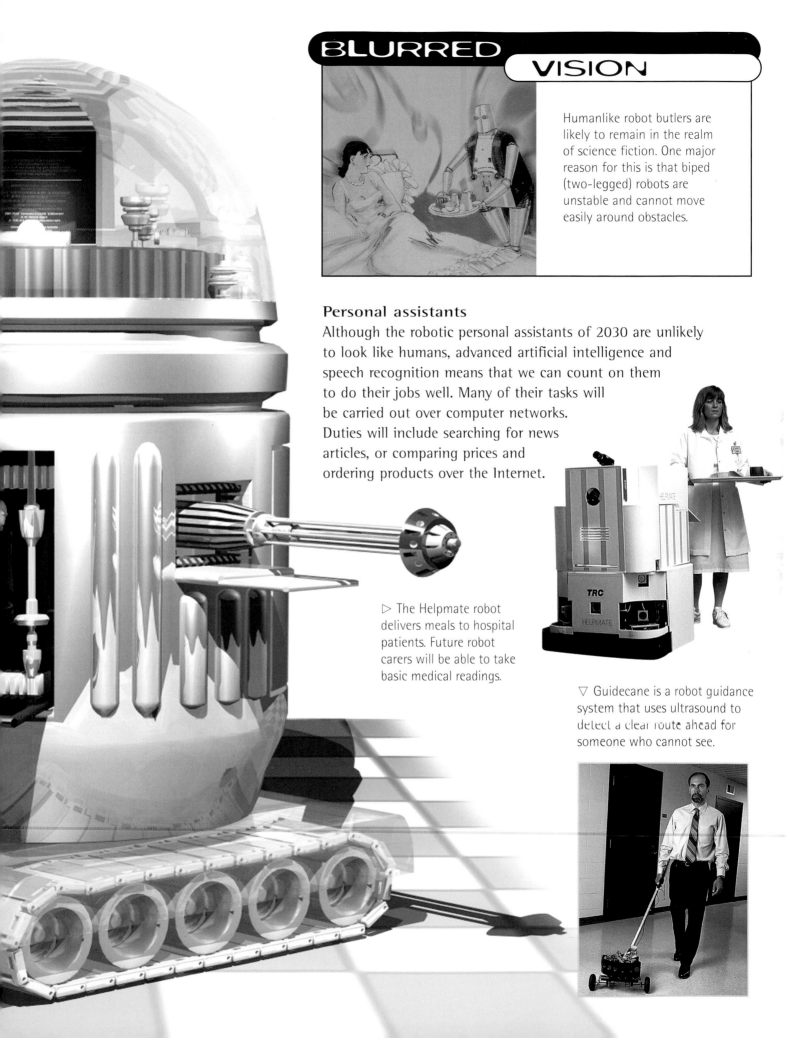

Humanlike robot butlers are likely to remain in the realm of science fiction. One major reason for this is that biped (two-legged) robots are unstable and cannot move easily around obstacles.

Personal assistants

Although the robotic personal assistants of 2030 are unlikely to look like humans, advanced artificial intelligence and speech recognition means that we can count on them to do their jobs well. Many of their tasks will be carried out over computer networks. Duties will include searching for news articles, or comparing prices and ordering products over the Internet.

▷ The Helpmate robot delivers meals to hospital patients. Future robot carers will be able to take basic medical readings.

▽ Guidecane is a robot guidance system that uses ultrasound to detect a clear route ahead for someone who cannot see.

▷ Before computers, banking was slow, time-consuming, and relied on sifting through vast amounts of paper records.

SHOPPING AND BANKING

Shopping, banking, and security will change dramatically during the 21st century. In the late 1990s, many communities had already moved toward electronic currency. Electronic money—in the form of microprocessors that hold a person's complete financial details—will eventually replace paper and coin money. Electronic currency and the growth of the Net for shopping will mean that financial transactions will be handled entirely by machines. This means that machines will need to be able to identify people. Security systems are most likely to be based on biometrics—the scientific measurement of a person's physical features.

Biometrics

Biometrics is expected to become one of the fastest growing industries in the first half of the 21st century. Biometrics uses the unique characteristics of the human voice or a particular part of the body—the face, finger, ear, or eye for example—to identify someone. A biometric system scans one or more of these features and then looks for a match, comparing the information with what is in its memory.

△ Each person's eye has unique features. Sensar is an iris scanning system that creates an eye print and looks for a perfect match in its memory.

Wallet replacement

How will the new electronic currencies be carried? The majority of our credit and financial details will be held in automatic machines that can be accessed using a biometric security system. Microprocessors attached to a smart card, or even implanted within the body, could hold financial records. These devices would also be capable of performing functions such as instant money conversion.

△ At the end of the 1990s, shopping over the Internet was still in its early stages. With improved security and virtual reality systems, shopping from home or local VR stations is expected to flourish by 2010.

△ This robot shopping cart uses ultrasound to follow a customer around the world's first automated department store, Seibu, in Japan.

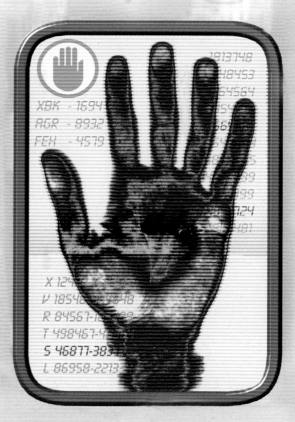

△ Electronic hand scanners could be in use in many countries by 2010.

◁ A user's eye is scanned by an automatic teller machine (ATM) of 2015. The machine may also check other aspects of your face or scan your hand before you are allowed to get money or account information.

Watching you

Like it or not, in the 21st century our lives may be constantly watched and many of our actions recorded. It will be possible to track a person's actions through their use of the Internet, credit cards, and smart cards. People will be watched more and more by advanced digital camera systems and closed circuit TV (CCTV). It is likely that the public will campaign to reduce the amount of intrusion into people's lives.

MACHINES IN HAZARDOUS AREAS

△ A bomb disposal robot approaches a bomb. It has a long-reaching robot arm with various tools attached for defusing bombs and controlling explosions.

Machines are the perfect tools for getting dangerous jobs done or for doing work in hazardous places. Machines have traveled to distant and hostile planets and deep into the depths of the ocean where no human explorers could survive. On land, machines perform jobs that we cannot do in places that we cannot go. Such no-go areas include sites where toxic chemicals and radioactivity are present, the insides of storage tanks and pipelines, and in and around volcanoes or fierce fires where the heat is intense. As the 21st century progresses, increasingly sophisticated hazard robots, or hazbots, will be developed from materials that are resistant to heat, shock, and other dangers.

Defusing the situation

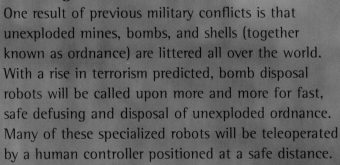

One result of previous military conflicts is that unexploded mines, bombs, and shells (together known as ordnance) are littered all over the world. With a rise in terrorism predicted, bomb disposal robots will be called upon more and more for fast, safe defusing and disposal of unexploded ordnance. Many of these specialized robots will be teleoperated by a human controller positioned at a safe distance.

▷ Future fire-fighting robots will use visual signals and sounds to lead people to escape exits. They will also provide oxygen masks, and spray water and other flame-extinguishing substances to cut a safe path through the fire.

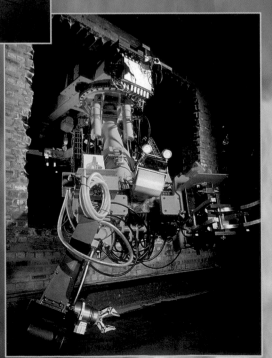

◁ Remote-controlled robot arms are common in the nuclear industry. A person uses hand controls to move the robot's arms. The robot, which is not affected by radiation, can make very precise movements.

Nuclear sites

Radioactivity is a threat to all living things. Machines made of inorganic metals and composites can handle high levels of radioactivity without being damaged and they are widely used in the nuclear industry. In the future, there will be a growing number of nuclear sites that will have to be taken down and made safe. Automated machines and robots will be essential in this process, known as decommissioning.

Fire-fighting robots

Despite the safeguards that will be built into future buildings, the risk of fire will always exist. Even sophisticated sprinkler systems may not work against a major blaze. By 2020, the use of fire-fighting robots will be standard practice in many places. These will use a range of heat sensors and an internal map of the building to find a way into the heart of the fire area. Once there, the robots will put out the fire with foams and other substances.

△ *Robug 3* is a robot that has the ability to scale walls and ceilings. It uses powerful suckers driven by compressed air to create a partial vacuum under each of its eight feet.

▽ *Dante* is an eight-legged robot designed to move over dangerous, unstable ground. It has successfully made its way into the mouth of the Alaskan volcano, Mt. Spurr.

UNDERWATER MACHINES

Over 70 percent of our planet is covered by water. Our seas and oceans not only contain marine life but also a huge supply of valuable minerals. As land-based resources become overstretched or exhausted, we will venture under water more and more in search of new supplies. We will also explore the oceans to keep watch on the oceans' ecosystems. Much of this work will be performed by unmanned intelligent machines called Autonomous Underwater Vehicles or AUVs.

△ Early diving equipment, such as the Klingart diving suit from the late 1700s, only worked at shallow depths.

△ A modern deep-sea diving apparatus encloses the diver in an ultratough shell, resistant in depths of up to 220 feet.

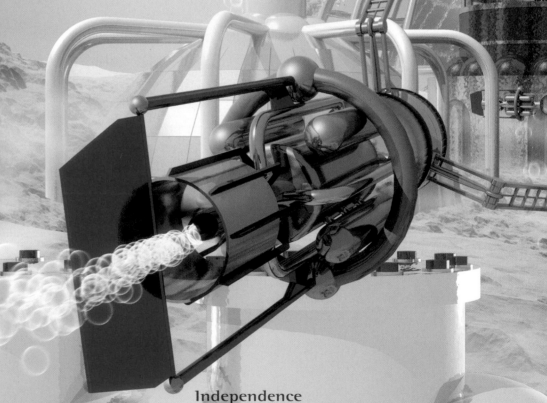

Machine advantages

One of the major problems faced by people exploring under water is that, the deeper you go, the greater the water pressure—the pressure doubles every 30 feet you go down. It is far easier to make unmanned machines that are capable of withstanding the immense pressures found at great depths. Unmanned machines are cheaper to build than manned machines, more maneuverable, and involve no risk to human life.

Independence

At present, Remote Operated Vehicles (ROVs) are controlled by a human operator on the surface and linked by a long cable called a tether. In the future, however, AUVs are likely to take over their role. Using complex sensor and control systems, these machines will operate without direct human control. By 2010, AUVs will be mapping the seabed as well as maintaining underwater cables and pipelines.

◁ Small underwater settlements, holding up to 30 people, may be with us by 2025. Samples of minerals, rocks, and living things will be collected by small, multiarmed machines. Core drillers will take samples from layers of rock.

△▷ *Jason Jr.* is an ROV controlled by operators aboard the manned submersible *Alvin. Jason Jr.* successfully investigated and photographed the wreck of the *Titanic*.

Mineral resources

It has been estimated that there are over 220 billion tons of minerals, including metals, in the Earth's seas and oceans. Manganese nodules, for example, litter many parts of the ocean floor. So far, it has not been practical to extract these types of materials from seawater. However, mining the oceans using AUVs and other machines is likely to prove far more effective.

Man vs. Machine?

Manned spacecraft allow firsthand human experience of space to be recorded, such as the effects of zero gravity on the human body and mind. However, there is no air, water, or food in space. It all has to be carried, along with living quarters for the astronauts. Spacecraft that can support life are more expensive and complex to build than unmanned probes, so a mixture of manned and unmanned missions is likely to continue long into the future.

△ The successor to the space shuttle will be based on the *X-33* and is scheduled for launch in 2005.

MACHINES IN SPACE 1

Without machines we would never have been able to leave the Earth and explore space. At first, unmanned space probes, launched by rockets, orbited the planet. Astronauts soon followed. These human pioneers relied on the most advanced machinery and technology of their time to keep them alive and get them home safely. Machines paved the way for further manned exploration, first to the moon, in preparation for the manned landings between 1969 and 1972, and then out into the solar system. A number of probes are currently traveling to the far reaches of the solar system and beyond.

△ The *Atlas–Mercury* rocket launched the United States' first manned spaceflight in 1962. Astronaut John Glenn orbited the planet three times before returning to Earth.

One-way ticket

Many unmanned machines have been sent into space with zero expectation of their recovery. Probes have been sent near the sun or onto hostile planet surfaces such as Mercury and Venus. Others have journeyed right through the solar system and out into deep space. Experiments and sensors on board the probes are designed to run automatically, sending back data via high-frequency radio waves.

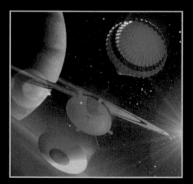

△ In November 2004, the *Huygens* probe will be dropped from the *Cassini* orbiter into the atmosphere of Titan, Saturn's largest moon.

◁ Launched in 1977, *Voyager 1* is now the most distant space probe, 6.5 billion miles away from the Earth. Radio signals sent by *Voyager* take almost 10 hours to reach the Earth.

◁ The *Apollo 11* mission in 1969 was the first to land men on the moon. They performed a range of experiments there.

The moon revisited

Scientific breakthroughs from the International Space Station (ISS) may spark renewed interest in the moon and the establishment of a permanent research colony there. Plans for a lunar observatory on the far side of the moon and a manned mission to Mars may provide the scientific motivation for building the colony. Huge multinational companies who might be interested in the rare minerals found on the moon may provide the sponsorship needed to make the colony a reality.

Space launches by 2100 may use incredibly high-powered lasers to heat the air below a craft to temperatures as high as 54,000°F. The thrust generated could be enough to propel the craft into orbit without rockets.

△ A permanent lunar base could be up and running before 2020. It will be constructed with the help of robots and is likely to be nuclear- or solar-powered.

MACHINES IN SPACE 2

Huge amounts of money, time, and effort are needed to send machines and people into space. The International Space Station (ISS), launched in 1998, marks a new age of joint international effort that is likely to kickstart a boom in space technology. Lessons learned from its design, construction, and operation will provide the basis for developing bigger and better space stations. The ISS and future stations will greatly increase our understanding of space science—especially the effects of microgravity, or weightlessness. This is likely to lead to the development of new materials and industrial processes.

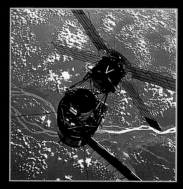

△ *Skylab*, launched in 1973, was America's first space station. It proved that humans could live and work in space for extended periods.

△ The Russian *Mir* space station, launched in 1986, is highly automated. Only 13 percent of its operations are done by human beings.

Stepping stone

The ISS is a joint project between 15 different countries, including the United States, Canada, Russia, Japan, and Britain. At least 45 missions will be involved in constructing the most ambitous man-made structure ever built in space. Powered by huge panels of solar cells and equipped with six laboratories, the ISS will provide more than a decade of active service after it is completed in 2004.

△ Working in space involves a combination of machines and astronauts equipped for extravehicular activity (EVA). Here, a satellite capturing device is attached to the end of a space shuttle's robot arm.

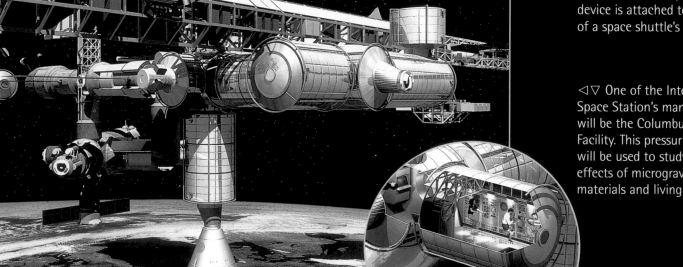

◁▽ One of the International Space Station's many features will be the Columbus Orbital Facility. This pressurized module will be used to study the effects of microgravity on materials and living matter.

▷ Rotating space hotels, shaped like bicycle wheels, may orbit Earth by 2040. The spinning motion will create artificial gravity in the outer wheel of the hotel.

All hands on deck

Building any structure in space creates unique problems. Components must be taken into space aboard shuttles and modules launched by rockets. Once in space, astronauts and robots need to work together. Teleoperated robot cameras travel around the site providing all-over views while robot grippers move parts into place. Future constructions will be assembled by robots working autonomously—without human help.

Alternative destination

The space program of the 1960s and 1970s led to many unexpected advances in mechanics, robotics, medicine, and computer development. Experiments that take place on future space stations are likely to lead to new areas of scientific research. Space stations could also be used as factories to manufacture new materials or, one day, as vacation spots for space tourists.

OUR NEW HOME

Much of the human race's drive into space has been to learn about the planets and moons that are the Earth's neighbors. From the *Apollo* moon landings to probes such as *Voyager* and *Mariner*, sent on flyby trajectories near the major planets, machines have been central to the exploration of other worlds. The planetary rovers and probes of the 1990s were mostly controlled by high frequency radio wave signals sent from mission control on Earth. Machines sent out to other planets after 2010 will be highly intelligent and able to act independently using information gathered by an array of sensors. The information that machines send back to the Earth will pave the way for manned missions to Mars from 2025 onward with the hope that, one day, we will be able to live on the planet.

△ *Viking I* was the very first manufactured object to land on the surface of another planet. It reached Mars in 1975 and took soil samples and pictures that were relayed back to mission control on Earth.

△In 1997, the *Sojourner* robot, carried by the *Pathfinder* probe, landed on Mars. *Sojourner* was instructed by radio signals sent from the Earth, but it also used its own sensors to find a route to a specified target area.

Biospheres

Closed ecology units, sometimes known as biospheres, may be sent to Mars first. These would be constructed by machines and robots before astronauts arrive to live inside them. The units would be closed off from the Martian environment, only taking in solar energy from outside. All wastes would be recycled, and oxygen would be generated using plants grown inside the unit.

△ Closed ecology units, such as the two-acre *Biosphere 2* in Arizona, have already been successfully built on Earth.

A suitable planet

Terraforming is the most ambitious of all future plans for settling on other planets. Terraforming means changing the entire environment of a planet and its atmosphere so that Earth plants and animals can live there. Mars, with its low atmospheric pressure and polar ice caps, is the most promising planet for terraforming.

Temperature rising

Mars needs to be warmed up and to have a thicker atmosphere created if the planet is to be terraformed. To achieve this, gases could be pumped into the Martian atmosphere to create a greenhouse effect that would trap more of the sun's heat. If frost and part of the polar ice caps can be melted, they will provide both water on the ground and water vapor in the atmosphere. Genetically engineered bacteria and microbes that absorb carbon dioxide and give out oxygen could be introduced. Although terraforming is a process that takes many thousands of years, we should not underestimate what the future will bring.

△ Thousands of years from now, terraforming might transform Mars, creating water reserves and a breathable atmosphere. Lightweight structures could take advantage of the low gravity, while unmanned machines could carry materials and perform maintenance work.

GLOSSARY

Alternative energies Any source of energy that does not rely on the burning of fossil fuels (gas, coal, and oil) or nuclear power. Alternative energies include solar, geothermal, and hydroelectric power.

Artificial Intelligence (AI) The ability of machines to do intelligent things, such as making decisions based on given information.

Autonomous Used to describe a machine, usually a robot, that does not depend on human control to perform all of its functions.

Biometrics The measurement of a person's unique anatomical features from finger- and handprints to eye and facial characteristics.

Composite materials Artificial materials that feature a mixture of different materials that are woven or bonded together.

Fuzzy logic A way for a computer to process information that is more like the way the human brain works than in a normal computer.

Geothermal power Power generated by using the heat that comes from deep inside the Earth.

Gravity The force of attraction between two bodies.

Laser A highly focused beam of light or other radiation, used to cut through objects or to carry information through fiber optics.

Microchip A small but complex electronic device in which millions of transistors and other components are mounted on a single slice of material, usually silicon, to form an integrated circuit.

Microprocessor A type of microchip that can be programmed to perform calculations or control machinery. Microprocessors are the thinking components in robots and computers.

Nanotechnology Technology created to work on a nanometric scale (nanometer=one billionth of a meter).

Nuclear fission Splitting the nucleus of an atom to generate enormous amounts of power.

Nuclear fusion Forcing atoms to collide and fuse together to generate vast amounts of power. Fusion takes place constantly in the sun's core.

Pneumatics A drive system that uses a gas such as air to provide power.

Radioactivity The release of electromagnetic energy, or radiation, from the nuclei of unstable atoms.

Recycling Making productive use of waste substances, for example, by making newspaper out of waste paper.

Renewable resources Materials and energies that can be used without risk of them running out. Examples of renewable resources include solar power, wave power, and crops.

Sensor A device that gives a computer or microprocessor information about its surroundings, such as temperature, sound, movement, or light.

SMA Shape memory alloy; a new material capable of remembering its original shape and returning to it after being handled.

Smart card A card with a built-in microprocessor that contains personal information and can be used for things like shopping and banking.

Smart machine A machine or system that uses sensors and a microprocessor to make it behave in an intelligent way, for example, by remembering or predicting a user's actions.

Stealth A collection of technologies that work together to make a vehicle (usually an aircraft) less detectable to radar and other forms of sensing.

Streamline To shape a machine or vehicle so that it travels through gases or liquids more smoothly and efficiently.

Superconductivity The ability of certain materials to conduct electricity with little resistance at very low temperatures.

Telecommunications The transmission and reception of information-carrying signals over a long distance. Telephone, radio, and television are familiar telecommunications systems.

Teleoperation A system that allows someone to control or operate a machine from a distance.

Terraforming The modification of the entire environment of a planet and its atmosphere to allow plants and animals from Earth to live there.

Transistor A small electronic switch that replaced the cumbersome and less reliable vacuum tubes in electric circuits and helped make small, powerful microchips possible.

Ultrasound A sensing system that uses very high frequency sounds that are outside the range of human hearing.

Virtual reality (VR) A system that uses computers to generate an artificial environment with which a human user can interact.

WEBSITES

There are many websites related to machines and technology and how they are likely to develop in the future.

If you are interested in learning more about nanotechnology and micromachinery, http://www.lucifer.com is a great starting point.

For an up-to-the-minute account of space shuttle missions and how construction of the International Space Station is progressing, visit NASA's official Space Station website at:
http://spaceflight.nasa.gov/station/index.html

Running since 1996, the Cool Robot Of The Week website sends you to the web pages of many of the leading robotics laboratories around the world. It can be found at:
http://ranier.hq.nasa.gov/telerobotics_page/coolrobots.html

MIT Labs have been at the forefront of machine and technology advances for decades. They publish an exciting and absorbing magazine called *Technology Review*. You can access the online version at:
http://www.techreview.com/currnt.htm

To find out more about anything related to robots, robotics, and automated machinery, look at the FAQ section of Carnegie–Mellon University's robotics pages at: http://www.frc.ri.cmu.edu/robotics-faq

A fascinating look at how terraforming on a planet such as Mars may be achieved can be found at:
http://www.concentric.net/~stysk/uststuff/terraform.htm

To keep up with news of the latest developments in technology and its future, try *Popular Science*'s website at: http://www.popsci.com

For an interesting and thought-provoking collection of insights into what the future might bring for power, machinery, and the way we live in the 21st century, head over to *21st Century Creative Alternatives*. The website can be found at:
http://web0.tiac.net/users/seeker/IT21stlinks.html

PLACES OF INTEREST

Many museums and science centers around the country have displays and exhibitions that highlight some of the latest and forthcoming developments in machines and technology.

The National Air and Space Museum (Washington D.C.) is part of the Smithsonian Institution. It has many galleries devoted to both the history of space flight and exploration, as well as exhibits and displays on what the future might bring.

The Museum of Science and Industry (Chicago, IL) is the oldest science museum in the Western hemisphere and the first in North America to have hands-on, interactive exhibits that explore all aspects of science and how it affects our lives.

The Space Center (Alamogordo, NM) celebrates all things related to space exploration. It aims to preserve and interpret the history, technology, and science of the Space Age.

The Computer Museum (Boston, MA) features a comprehensive history of computers that looks at their evolution, technology, and impact, as well as exhibits on robots and networks.

The California Science Center (Los Angeles, CA) features the *Creative World* which examines how humans have built structures and machines to enhance their environment.

The Tech Museum of Innovation (San Jose, CA) has over 240 interactive, hands-on exhibits about the technologies that affect our daily lives.

Finally, **The Cyberspace Museum of Natural History & Exploration Technology** offers information on a variety of subjects, including space exploration. It can also point you toward other (real) museums that have related exhibitions. You can find it at:
http://www.cyberspacemuseum.com

INDEX

A

aircraft 32–33, 34, 35, 38, 39, 40
Alvin submersible 53
Apollo 11 mission 54
artificial intelligence (AI) 11, 13, 47, 60
assembly lines 8, 11, 12, 13
atomic bomb 32
atoms 16, 18, 24–25
automatons 10
automatic guided vehicles (AGVs) 13
automatic teller machines (ATMs) 49
automation 9, 12, 42
autonomous underwater vehicles (AUVs) 52, 53

B

banking 48–49
batteries 20, 30, 31, 44
battlegrounds 40–41
biofuel 20, 22
biometrics 36, 48, 49, 60
biospheres 58, 59
body armor 36, 41
bombs 32, 39, 50
Buckminsterfullerene 18

C

cameras 34, 57
camouflage 41
cannons 32, 36
Čapek, Karel 10
cars 13, 15, 16, 26
CCGT (combined cycle gas turbine) 22
Chernobyl 24
climate control 44, 45, 58–59
closed-circuit TV (CCTV) 49
coal 22
communications systems 41, 42, 44, 46
composite materials 8, 18, 19, 30, 36, 51, 60

D

computational fluid dynamics (CFD) 30
computers 15, 20, 30, 31, 35, 46
credit cards 43, 49

D

defense 34–35, 37
Denmark 28
diving apparatus 52
domestic machines 44–47
drilling 22, 23, 27, 53

E

efficiency 30–31
electricity 20, 23, 26, 27, 28, 29, 31
electromagnets 24, 31
electronic currency 48, 49
electronic tagging 34
electrotextiles 19, 44
elite forces 41
environmental concerns 17, 22, 24, 25, 29, 30
extravehicular activity (EVA) 56

F

fabrics 18, 19
factories 9, 12–13, 57
fast breeder reactors 25
fiberglass 19
fire fighting 50, 51
food technology 44, 45
fossil fuels 22–23
friction 30, 31
Fuller, R. Buckminster 18

G

gas 22, 23
geothermal power 27, 60
glass, smart 45
glass-reinforced plastic (GRP) 18
Glenn, John 54
gravity 54, 56, 57, 59, 60
guidance systems 47
Guidecane 47
gunpowder 32, 36
guns 32, 36, 37

H

hand scanners 49
Hoover Dam 28
Hot Dry Rock (HDR) technology 27
hydroelectric power 28

I

Iceland 27
identification 48, 49
image resolution 34, 35
industry 8–19
integrated circuits 14
internal combustion engine 20
International Space Station (ISS) 55, 56
Internet 34, 47, 48, 49
iris scanning systems 48, 49

J

Jason Jr. ROV 53
Joint European Torus project 25
Joint Strike Fighter 38

K

Kevlar 18, 36
kinetic energy 20
kitchens 44, 45

L

lasers 25, 37, 55, 60
lawn mowers 46
Lockheed *B2* bomber 35
Lycra 18

M

machine guns 36
Magnetic Levitation (Maglev) 31
Mars 43, 55, 58–59
mass production 8, 12, 13
materials 8, 18–19, 30, 31, 36, 51, 57
Maxim Mk1 machine gun 36
medical care 9, 16, 17, 46, 47
Merkle, Ralph 16
metals 9, 18, 19, 30, 51, 53
micromachines 14–15, 34
MicroElectroMechanical systems (MEMs) 14
microprocessors 36, 44, 49, 60
microwave ovens 43, 44

military machines 32–39
mineral resources 53
mining 22, 23, 53
Mir space station 56
molecules 9, 16
money 48, 49
moon 23, 43, 54, 55, 57

N

nanotechnology 16–17, 60
NASA (National Aeronautics and
  Space Administration) 19, 35
neural networking 11
neutrons 24
night vision goggles 36, 41
nuclear power 9, 20, 24–25, 50, 51
  fission 24, 25, 60
  fusion 19, 24, 25, 26, 60
  reactors 20, 25
nylon 18

O

offices 15, 19, 46
oil 17, 18, 22, 23

P

perpetual motion machine 31
Persian Gulf War 39
personal assistants 46, 47
photovoltaic cells 20, 26
plastics 18, 19, 22
pollution 17, 22, 24, 25, 26
power 20–22
  electricity 20, 23, 26, 27, 28,
    29, 31
  fossil fuels 22–23
  geothermal 27
  hydroelectric 28
  nuclear 9, 20, 24–25, 50, 51
  solar 17, 20, 26, 27, 36, 44, 58
  steam 20, 26, 27
  tidal 28, 29
  wave 20, 29
  wind 28, 29
power plants 20, 22, 24–25, 42

R

radar 34, 35, 39
radioactivity 24, 25, 51, 60
recycling 44, 58, 60
remote operated vehicles (ROVs)

52, 53
remote operations 9, 13, 22, 23, 27,
  35, 42, 52
revolvers 32
Richtofen, Baron von 38
robotics 10–11, 15, 57
robots 10–11, 13
  bomb disposal 50
  carers 46, 47
  COG 11
  Dante 51
  delivery systems 39
  domestic 43, 46–47
  fire-fighting 50, 51
  hazbots 50–51
  helicopters 14
  home tutors 46
  incendiary 33, 38, 39
  industrial 8, 9, 13, 46, 50
  infantry 41
  insect 38, 39
  lawn mowers 46
  maintenance 13, 23, 27
  many-robot systems 15
  nanobots 9, 17
  personal assistants 46, 47
  Robart III 37
  Robug 3 51
  shopping 42, 49
  Sojourner 58
rockets 39, 54, 55, 57
Rossum's Universal Robots 10

S

safety devices 36, 37
satellites 33, 34, 35, 43, 56
secret agents 34
security systems 44, 48, 49
shape memory alloys (SMAs) 9, 19,
  45
shopping 13, 42, 48–49
S.I.G. assault rifles 37
silica aerogel 19
silicon 14, 19
Skylab 56
smart cards 49, 60
smart materials 8, 19, 44
Sojourner robot 58
solar power 17, 20, 26, 27, 36,
  44, 58
space hotels 42, 57

space probes 43, 54, 57, 58
space shuttles 54, 57
space stations 43, 55–56, 57
spacecraft 54–57
speech recognition 15, 47
spying 34–35, 49
stainless steel 8
stealth technology 33, 34, 35, 36,
  38, 39, 60
steam power 20, 26, 27
sticky guns 37
streamlining 30, 31
superconductivity 19, 31, 60
surgery 9, 16, 17

T

terraforming 59, 60
tidal power 28, 29
tokamaks 24, 25
torpedoes 32
transistors 14, 60
troops 40, 41
turbines 22, 26, 28, 29

U

ultrasound 47, 49, 60
underwater machines 52–53
underwater settlements 53
Unimate robot 8, 10
unmanned aerial vehicles (UAVs) 35

V

Viking I 58
virtual reality 9, 49, 60
visors 15, 41
vitrification 25
volcanoes 27, 51
Volta, Alessandro 30
voltaic piles 30
Voyager 1 54, 58

W

waterwheels 20, 28
wave power 20, 29
weapons 32–33, 36–37
wind farms 28, 29
World War I 38, 40
World War II 39, 40

X

X-33 spacecraft 54

ACKNOWLEDGMENTS

The publishers would like to thank the following illustrators for
their contribution to this book:

Arcana 40–41; **Julian Baum** 14–15, 16–17, 27 c, 52–53, 54 br
58–59; **Graham Humphries** 19 tr, 23 tr, 44 br, 55 tr; **Alex Pang** 10–11,
22–23, 24–25, 28–29, 38–39, 46–47, 56–57; **Mark Preston** 6–7,
8–9, 12–13, 19 c, 20–21, 32–33, 42–43, 48–49.

The publishers would like to thank the
following for supplying photographs:

Cover (*front*) cl Science Photo Library/600 Group Fanuc/David
Parker tl Science Photo Library/Sam Ogden; Cover (back) br
Science Photo Library/Brian Brake; 6 c Science Photo
Library/Sam Ogden, br Science Photo Library/Brian Brake; 8 tl
Science Photo Library/600 Group Fanuc/David Parker, tr Sylvia
Corday Photo Library Ltd, cl Mary Evans Picture Library, c
Science & Society Picture Library/Science Museum, cr Hulton
Getty (*car*), cr Science & Society Picture Library; 9 tl Xerox
PARC/Dr. K. Eric Drexler and Dr. Ralph Merkle, tr Science Photo
Library/Sam Ogden, cl Science Photo Library/Brian Brake; 10 tl
The Bridgeman Art Library/Private Collection, bl Hulton Getty;
11 tr Science Photo Library/Brian Brake, c J.S. Automation, br
Science Photo Library/Sam Ogden; 12 bl The Bridgeman Art
Library/Private Collection; 13 t Science Photo Library/Peter
Menzel, b The Ronald Grant Archive; 14 tl Science & Society
Picture Library, tr Science Photo Library/Tony Craddock; 15 tl
Institut für Mikrotechnik, Mainz GmbH, Germany, tr Science
Photo Library/Manfred Kage; 16 tl Moorfields Eye Hospital, bl
IBM, br Xerox PARC/Dr. K. Eric Drexler and Dr. Ralph Merkle; 18
tl Science Photo Library/Ken Eward, tr Science Photo Library/Ken
Eward, cl Mary Evans Picture Library, br Tony Stone
Images/Dennis O'Clair; 19 tl Science Photo Library/Eye of
Science, bc Science Photo Library/Peter Menzel, br Science Photo
Library/Ken Eward; 20 c Science Photo Library/Martin Bond, bl
Science & Society Picture Library/Science Museum, br Mary
Evans Picture Library; 22 cr Environmental Images/Martin Bond,
tl Still Pictures, cl Hutchinson Library; 23 tl Science Photo
Library/D.A. Peel; 24 tl Hulton Getty; 25 tl JET Joint
Undertaking, cr Frank Spooner Pictures/Gamma-Liaison, bl
Science Photo Library/Martin Bond, br Mary Evans Picture
Library; 26 tl Camera Press/Ralph Crane, cl Science Photo
Library/Martin Bond, cr Science Photo Library/Alex Bartel, br
Honda (U.K.); 26–27 b Science Photo Library/Tommaso
Guicciardini; 27 t Geoscience Features Picture Library; 28 tl The
Bridgeman Art Library/Fitzwilliam Museum, University of
Cambridge, cl Rex Features, bl Science Photo Library/David
Parker; 29 tl Science Photo Library/Martin Bond; 30 tl Science &
Society Picture Library/Science Museum/Clive Streeter, bl Frank
Spooner Pictures/Gamma-Liaison; 30–31 c Science Photo
Library/NASA, 31 t Mary Evans Picture Library, cr Science &
Society Picture Library/National Railway Museum, bc Science &
Society Picture Library/Bousfield/BKK, br Science Photo
Library/Chemical Design Ltd., 32 c Science Photo Library/Beinat,
Jerrican, cr TRH/NASM, r Science Photo Library/U.S. Navy, bl
Hulton Getty, (*revolve*) ET Archive, bc Science Photo Library, 32–
33 b Science Photo Library/Beinat, Jerrican, 33 cl The Aviation

Picture Library/Austin J. Brown, c TRH/NASM, br /B. Kraft; 34 tl
Camera Press/Vario-Press, cl Rex Features/Peter Brooker, cr
Corbis U.K./Everett, bl Science Photo Library/David Ducros; 35 t
The Aviation Picture Library/Austin J. Brown, cl CCS
Communication Control System Ltd., bl Tony Stone Images/Chad
Slattery, bc Tony Stone Images/Dennis O'Clair, br Tony Stone
Images/Dennis O'Clair; 36 t TRH, cl Science & Society Picture
Library, cr TRH/Armourshield Ltd., bl Frank Spooner Pictures;
36–37 br Frank Spooner Pictures/J.M. Turpin; 37 t Photo Press,
The Defence Picture Library, cl Rex Features/Dennis Cameron, tc
(*bullet*) Jaycor, bc Rex Features/Dennis Cameron, bl SPAWAR, br
Science & Society Picture Library; 38 tl Northrop Grumman
Corporation, cl Hulton Getty; 39 tc Frank Spooner Pictures
/Gamma, tr Frank Spooner Pictures/Gamma; 40 tl TRH/Imperial
War Museum; 41 tl The Aviation Picture Library/Matra Systemes
& Information, tr Frank Spooner Pictures/Gamma, cl TRH/
Thomson-CSF, 43 cl Frank Spooner Pictures/Charles/Liaison,
(*Satellite*) Camera Press; cl NASA, cr Diners Club International,
(*Sputnik*) Science Photo Library/Novosti; 44 c Frank Spooner
Pictures/Liaison, bl Philips/Visions of the Future; 45 cr
Softroom/Design: J. Jones/T. Spencer, b /Design: J. Jones/ T.
Spencer, 46 tl Frank Spooner Pictures/Gamma-Liaison, cl Science
Photo Library/Hank Morgan, 47 tc Mary Evans Picture Library,
cr Science Photo Library/Hank Morgan, br Science Photo
Library/Peter Yates; 48 tc Hulton Getty; c Frank Spooner
Pictures/Gamma-Liaison; 49 tr Frank Spooner Pictures/Gamma-
Liaison, c Science Photo Library/Jerrican Daudier; 50 tl Science
Photo Library/Spencer Grant, cl Science Photo Library/Hank
Morgan, b BNFL; 51 t Frank Spooner Pictures/FSP/Gamma/Tom
Kidd, b NASA Ames Research Center; 52 tl Mary Evans Picture
Library; 53 tr Frank Spooner Pictures/Gamma-Liaison, cr Frank
Spooner Pictures/Gamma-Liaison; 54 tr Lockheed Martin, cl
Science Photo Library/NASA, b NASA; 55 b Science Photo
Library/Victor Habbick Visions; 56 tl Science Photo
Library/NASA, cl Science Photo Library/NASA, cr Science Photo
Library/NASA, bl Science Photo Library/David Ducros, bc Science
Photo Library/David Ducros; 58 tl Science Photo Library; 59 tc
Science Photo Library/Peter Menzel.

Key: b = bottom, c = center, l = left, r = right, t = top.

Every effort has been made to trace the copyright holders
of the photographs. The publishers apologize for any
inconvenience caused.

The publishers would also like to thank the following:
Martin Cross, Keith Goodall of Stantec, Robert Kemp,
Gerhart Meurer of Johns Hopkins University, Dr. Andrew
Rudge of BNFL, and Michael White.